ENGAGE!

Essays on the Path to Higher Productivity through Effective Employee Communications

By PDP President Louise Dickmeyer
as well as PDP staff and team members

Copyright © 2014 PDP Solutions
All rights reserved.

NOTE TO THE READER

We hope you enjoy this collection of essays, written by the president of PDP Solutions Lou Dickmeyer, our resident internal communications specialist Liam Scanlan, as well as other PDP team members and partners.

The essays do not need to be read in any particular order.

If you wish to pursue more details behind any essay, for example, to follow links to publications we cite in an essay, you can search for that essay on our website (pdpsolutions.com) using any part of the essay title.

Thank you for investing your precious time into reading some or all of this book. We'd love to hear your thoughts, and I personally look forward to connecting with you when the subject of Internal Communication or Employee Engagement is on your mind.

Louise Dickmeyer
President, PDP Solutions

CONTENTS

1	FORWARD
3	PROLOGUE
5	ESSAYS
5	Business Values Follow Society's Values: Internal Communication in the Age of Social Transparency
8	Employee Information Kiosks: An Integral Part of Every Internal Communications System
10	What Happens When Employee Communication is Missing?
12	Ten Things I am Thankful for as we Approach Thanksgiving
13	Without Effective Employee Communications, Employees are Frozen in Time
16	Employee Communication: Connected at Home, so why not Connected at Work?
17	Employee Disengagement Can Do More Damage Than It's Worth
20	The Cookie Thief: Keeping Employees Engaged Means Being Aware Of What They Do For You
22	Employee Engagement: Five Reasons To Thank Your Front Line Employees
25	Gratitude: The Quickest Path to Full Employee Engagement
28	Employee Engagement is Required to Build Today's Complex Products

- 30 The Dichotomy—or "Catch 22"—of Poor Internal Communication
- 32 Making Employee Communication More Effective, Transparent and Fun
- 34 Employee Communications: The What, the How and the Why
- 35 Employee Communications: Transparency Every Company Should Have
- 37 Making Changes for Improved Employee Engagement
- 39 Internal Communications: Nature Always Wins
- 41 Internal Communication: Getting a Company Into Ship Shape Opens Interesting Doors
- 44 Employee Engagement: Soliciting the Help of Goats
- 46 Employee Engagement. It's What People Do All Day
- 48 Internal Communication and the Daily Act of Brushing One's Teeth
- 50 Internal Communications: From The Top, Down or From The Bottom, Up?
- 53 The Lack of Internal Communications is Reason #3 Why Companies Make Poor Products
- 55 Employee Engagement: Can't I Just Let My Supervisors Handle It?
- 58 Employee Engagement: The Good, the Bad and the Ugly
- 61 Employee Engagement and its Link to Double-Digit Growth
- 64 Competitiveness: Why Internal Communication is the Best Way to Compete in Your Market
- 67 Engaged Employees Have a Far Higher Retention Rate Than Disengaged Employees

69	The Importance of Internal Communication to Every Business
71	Internal Communications and why the Neanderthals Disappeared
72	Internal Communications: Coming to a Workplace Near You
74	Internal Communication: Why Every Company Must Get it Right
75	Internal Communication: Pivotal to Turning Around a Rundown Company
78	Internal Communications: Five Things Every SME Should Know
79	Getting the Message Through with Internal Communication
81	Excellent Internal Communication, and Other Habits You Never Want to Lose
82	Internal Communications: "That's a Human Resources Thing, isn't it?"
83	Internal Communications: The Decisive Factor in Survival of the Fittest
85	Employee Engagement: Why recognition is a key ingredient
87	Internal Communications Tools: The Sticky Way to Retain Your Productive Employees
88	Five Direct Benefits of Using a Modern Internal Communications Solution
90	Kiosks are Reemerging as a Cost Effective Component of the Modern Internal Communications Solution
91	Internal Communications and Why Leading Companies Embrace it

- 94   People over Processes: How Internal Communications Makes an Organization More Productive
- 96   Without a Foundation of Internal Communications, Human Resources Becomes Whack-a-Mole
- 98   Internal Communications Solutions: Did Someone call it Social Media?
- 100 How Internal Communications is the Gift that Keeps on Giving
- 102 Internal Communication in the Workplace: Will the Real Team Members Please Step Forward
- 103 Asabiyyah - The "glue" that is Internal Communication
- 105 Employee Communication and Industrial Secrecy
- 109 Human Resources' Greatest Value may be in Introducing an Internal Communications Solution
- 111 Do your Employees Hate You? Internal Communications offers a Path Forward
- 113 Employee Engagement and Owning Your Culture
- 115 The Holy Grail of Internal Communication: Knowing What to Focus on
- 117 Engaged Employees Six Ways to Get Your Employees Engaged Again
- 119 Employee Engagement and How to Become More Competitive
- 120 Employee Engagement: Why Alan Watts' Perspective is Right on the Money
- 121 Employee Information Kiosks are Here to Stay
- 123 Employee Information Kiosks: Keeping Up with the Latest in Employee Engagement
- 124 Employee Engagement: Internal Communications Solutions are a Recruitment Tool

- 125 Employee Engagement and the "Pull" Power of Employee Information Kiosks
- 127 Internal Communication: Ask and You Shall Receive
- 129 Satisfied Employees are there to get; Engaged Employees are there to give
- 130 The Relationship Between Recruiting and Employee Engagement
- 132 Employee Engagement - Show me the Money
- 133 Is your Employee Engagement Culture a Desert or Rainforest?
- 135 Employee Engagement feeds Productivity which feeds Employee Engagement
- 136 Employee Engagement - For Some, it's Still a Long Way to Go
- 141 Employee Communication and Industrial Secrecy
- 143 Successful Employee Engagement is made of a "Thousand Small Wins"
- 145 On the Adoption and Acceptance of Touchscreen Technology
- 146 Internal Communication. When you are your own worst enemy
- 149 Increasing ProductivityInternal Communications: Ten Free Ways to Get Started

FORWARD

Companies the world over face a new and gathering challenge. As manufacturing, service and product development become ever more complex atop a wave of technological advances, the demand for excellence in front line employees is growing in parallel. To remain competitive, every company is faced with the need to manage these new, complex environments, if it is to engage employees and raise productivity. In many cases, adaption might even be a requirement for survival, and not simply for higher profits.

The risk is to be left behind, leaving the spoils of economic growth and progress to those competitors who embraced this New Age of Employee Communication, Engagement and the productivity it delivers.

What is Employee Communication? Aren't email and PowerPoint slide shows enough to keep everyone in the loop? Don't we pay employees enough to get on with the job? Why must I, the CEO, be so involved when I have hired a human resources professional to take care of employees?

Internal Communication -- also called Employee Communication -- is more than email, PowerPoint and meetings. Those tools continue to play their part, but a complete internal communication system allows for full participation by employees from the front line all the way to the person at the top of the org chart. An unobstructed channel for transporting great ideas to that part of the organization where the decision can be made is a core element for success. Automatic feeds between dynamic corporate data and digital signage available to non-desk employees mean everyone gets the information they need to be successful in their job.

Together, these pivotal elements of an Internal Communication solution increase employee engagement, and improve productivity across the board.

In this book, we have gathered essays on the topics of internal communication, employee engagement, and digital signage, and how they feed into greater productivity. Written by members of the PDP team, they are not in any particular order. Each contains the URL tying it back to its respective blog posting, should you care to see a video or other link it refers to.

We hope this book helps you make a winning case for a robust internal communications solution in your own organization. Whether you are a CEO, a HR manager, or a front line employee who has a vision for a better way of working, this will surely feed that vision with facts behind the theories, and many ideas about how to make employee communication excellence a reality wherever you work.

And if you need our help, we are but a phone call away.

To Bold Moves!

Louise Dickmeyer
President, PDP Solutions

PROLOGUE

People Driven Performance came to life from my experiences over decades of running the Dotson Foundry. I learned the value of robust internal communication, engaged employees and the profound effect they have on productivity. In our case, it might have even been a matter of life or death for the company. It was economic crisis that woke me and my team up to what was possible when we took our own bold steps.

I hope you enjoy this collection of essays penned by members of the PDP team. It reflects the values we at PDP live by every day, and the dedication we have to our valued clients.

If you are already a client of ours, you know what I speak of. If not, I hope this will instill in you the same inspiration I felt years ago when I discovered the power of well implemented internal communication.

Choose a couple of essays you think you will like, and I invite you to call me personally if it resonates with your own experiences. If it does, we know we can help, and I look forward to calling you one of our own when the time is right for you.

Denny Dotson
Founder of PDP Solutions

ESSAYS

Business Values Follow Society's Values: Internal Communication in the Age of Social Transparency

If art mimics reality, then surely business mimics society as it reaches for more transparency in the workplace.

FIRST PUBLISHED NOV 8, 2013

Two generations ago, interpersonal communication was not a big priority. Married couples knew what they had to do, and got to it. The husband went to work, the wife stayed at home, and the business of family-making was executed with few words spoken.

Today's personal relationships demand a far higher rate of interpersonal communication than they did a generation ago.

For more reasons than I could list here, people grew to need more information. It enhanced their lives and their ability to contribute more meaningfully to their relationships. Today, we want to know how our partner feels, we want to express our own feelings and want to know more about our partner's needs, as well as wishing to express our own needs. Everything from personal hygiene to management of in-laws is now up for discussion. We are no longer willing to live in a take-it-or-leave-it world; everything is up for discussion and/or negotiation, and life is better for everyone as a result of our new world order of communication.

Work life mimics private life

For most people, work life is the second biggest personal commitment they make in their life; the first being commitment to a spouse or significant other, if they have one. I say work life is the second biggest only to marriage (I use the term 'marriage' here to cover any 'significant other' relationship) because it is relatively easy to unwind one's self from a job. True, you can always "find another job", but it is almost always a Major Event in one's life; one we remember for the rest of our life. And with it, comes stress, risk, uncertainty and loss of established personal connections. Perhaps the new job won't work out as we thought it would, or we might learn something about the new employer's viability only when we've worked there for a month.

From a financial or resource point of view, it could be argued that one's job takes priority over one's private life, because you need an income to fuel your private life.

OK, so we've established that the significance of a person's work life is of a similar order of magnitude to that of one's spousal commitment. And the relationship to one's work and one's colleagues is pivotal to the success of it, right? Few of us work in a conveyor belt type of job today; automation and overseas outsourcing has taken care of most of that. Instead, we work with people and processes. To be effective in the typical job of today, we have to know why we do work the way we do, where we personally fit in the organization, and we must have the means to communicate in two directions with the organization's leadership. Our work life now mimics our private life. It has just taken a bit of time for the former to catch up with the latter.

Setting expectations

Disappointment in many marriages stems from a mismatch of expectations. One spouse thought the other was going to provide such-and-such, but it didn't happen. If each knew what the other had expected, a failing relationship could have been rescued years before everyone felt so let down!

The primary role of communication in a relationship is to set expectations.

In our work lives, employee communication provides the same function: to set expectations. It's not just about what the company expects from an employee — which of course the employee must understand — but it is also about what the employee needs to satisfy those expectations. The employer needs a way to hear the word from the employee. And that, for most companies, comes in the form of an internal communications solution.

Communication = Success

Couples who have mastered the fine art of interpersonal communication, it is widely understood, have higher rates of relationship success. It's the same with companies. Those companies with robust internal communication have more engaged employees, higher employee retention and higher productivity.

That's how we help our clients every day, and we know you'd expect nothing less.

See more at: http://about.pdpsolutions.com/blog/business-values-follow-societys-values-internal-co.shtml

2

Employee Information Kiosks: An Integral Part of Every Internal Communications System

The rise of the self-serve, touch-screen employee information kiosk is well and truly underway.

FIRST PUBLISHED NOV 7, 2013

Do you find that technology has a habit of creeping up on you? It seems, the most effective technologies work their way into our lives without ever being formally introduced. For example, when the original ATMs came out in the late 1970s and early 1980s, they were so useful, we simply used them without any internal resistance. It's Friday night in town and you need twenty dollars for a car ride home? ATM to the rescue!

A single employee information kiosk can be shared by potentially hundreds of employees. Sometimes, one employee "drives" while her colleagues look on. This makes them very economical workplace information vehicles.

ATMs have come a long way since then. You can deposit cash or checks into them now. You can do a variety of other transactions to manage your account, transfer money, pay bills, and lots of other things. And then there's the worldwide aspect to it. You can withdraw cash from your Bank of America account using an ATM on a remote island in the Philippines. We're certainly not in Kansas anymore, Toto.

Smart phones, too, offer such a compelling set of features, they are almost irresistible. If you told me in 1977 that some time in the future I might spend $500 on a phone that would only last a few years, I would not have believed you.

But today, my smart phone can help me navigate my way across the city, share photos with friends, and look up recipes. It even lets me speak with other people far away!

Employee information kiosks are one of those technologies that have crept up on us. Properly implemented, they often require no significant training for first-time users. Their usefulness can be so compelling, employees take to them immediately. And once they get a taste of the type of information they provide, an engaged employee cannot go back to living without them.

I work on my laptop for many hours of the day. It's the nature of the "personal computer" that most employees who use one have one all to themselves. That makes complete sense for information workers like myself, but what about employees who spend most of their day doing … well … actual work? This is where a shared device makes more sense than a dedicated, one-person-only machine. For most non-desk employees, a few minutes a day might be enough time for them to get the information they need to help them do their job. In fact, it's often the case that several employees will use the PDP information kiosk at the same time. One employee "drives" while his or her colleagues look on. It's a great way to transfer know-how between employees, and it's also far more productive than water-cooler chit-chat.

See more at: http://about.pdpsolutions.com/blog/employee-information-kiosks-an-integral-part-of-ev.shtml

3

What Happens When Employee Communication is Missing?

It's unreasonable to expect employees to work everything out on their own. An organization without employee communication dies quietly from the inside out.

FIRST PUBLISHED NOV 6, 2013

If high blood pressure is the silent killer of the middle-aged man, then lack of communication must be the silent killer of the average company. Just imagine a team of front line employees who were disconnected from management. It would be a free-for-all, and management would never hear about important issues until they boiled over.

It's never too late if you start today

It's not too late to address internal communications issues ... if you start today!

For sure, the longer you wait to address internal communication problems, the more challenging it is likely to be for you. Unlike the middle-aged man who might give himself a heart attack by overexercising on the first day back at the gym, your company will feel the benefits of your first steps today. No heart attack required. What are those first steps? Lock your computer screen, place your smart phone in a drawer, and take a walk to your front line employees before you talk yourself out of it.

Mistaking the Urgent for the Important

Ten years ago, I had let myself go for a number of years. Between software product deadlines and taking care of my own children, good exercise had taken a bit of a back seat. Instead of going to gym, I was going out to dinner with prospects, or eating in an airport cafeteria. There was always something urgent to take care of, and I had mistaken the Urgent for the Important. I forgot what my father had told me many times: It's not a delay to stop and sharpen the scythe. After my first real cardiovascular workout in about seven years, I couldn't even lift my arms to grab the steering wheel to drive myself home. I determined then never to let myself go like that again.

When we meet a prospect for the first time at PDP, a common story we hear is, we were so busy taking care of what was urgent, we forgot some important things. Often, too, neglect of internal communication happens in companies during a period of tremendous growth. Employees and management might be overstretched managing big opportunities in front of them, and less urgent tasks can get neglected. Internal communication is a common casualty under such circumstances.

Sooner or later, though, especially when a company is growing, employee communication must be taken care of. The good news is, just like getting exercise, even a little of it is better than none at all. If you strike up a conversation with your front line staff today, you'll have accomplished the hardest part: getting started.

One of our clients used to have one or two meetings with their front line staff per year. After the PDP solution was up and running, they were communicating with their front line staff on a daily basis.

If you're still wondering how you might be able to get moving, we can help. We can give you a person-to-person online demonstration of our solution, or you can start right away with our sample questionnaire for your employees.

See more at: http://about.pdpsolutions.com/blog/what-happens-when-employee-communication-is-missin.shtml

Ten Things I am Thankful for as we Approach Thanksgiving
My reflections on how grateful I am for what's happening in the PDP universe.

FIRST PUBLISHED NOV 5, 2013

I am just getting back in the swing of offering blog posts in our ongoing efforts to enlighten employers about the positive effects of engaged employees and the use of effective internal communications.

Rather than writing something up, let me offer a couple of things I am thankful for regarding PDP.

I am so thankful for:

1. The incredibly positive response we got recently from HR managers and directors, business owners and senior executives on the PDP tools and approach.
2. Our growing list of clients!
3. The economy is picking up; that theme is being shared more widely every day, even if we still have a ways to go – that are getting better each day!
4. The creativity of clients and their use of PDP in their companies to communicate among one another.
5. The adoption and use of the tools by everyone from the CEO's office to some great front line staff members who are communicating in a new and enthusi-

astic way.
6. New cost effective and cool touchscreen hardware options as technology continues to evolve quickly in the marketplace.
7. Jazzy new version of our technology tools and looking forward to the full out launch.
8. The growing realization by clients and prospects that internal communications is a zero sum game when weighing PDP vs. what they have been doing. We are SOOO much better and more cost effective at the end of the day.
9. PDP is resonating with smaller organizations as well as some of the world's largest manufacturers. How fun is that?!!
10. Exciting new features that are under development as I write – so stay tuned for more!!

To Bold Moves!

See more at: http://about.pdpsolutions.com/blog/10-things.shtml

Without Effective Employee Communications, Employees are Frozen in Time

Employee communication is the foundation of a productive work culture. Here's why.

FIRST PUBLISHED NOV 4, 2013

An isolated employee is less capable and less likely to embrace change in the organization.

Under threat or under pressure, people tend to lean on their cultural values for support. Whether it's small groups of immigrants holding tightly onto traditions they brought with them from the Old Country, or individuals in a work environment who feel isolated from what's going on, humans under pressure are less likely to adapt to unfamiliar and new ideas, and more likely to stick to whatever worked in the past.

Pockets of European cultures that emigrated to North America took with them traditions they continued to protect and practice, while back home, the culture in their country of origin continued to change and evolve, as all cultures do when they have the power of self-determination.

While no society is perfectly democratic or perfectly fair, the United States has taken huge strides towards equality and equal opportunity in the last one hundred years. It wasn't always so. Earlier generations of immigrants had a tough time, so they preserved their "Irishness" or "Polishness" or "Germanness" as best they could. They kept in their hearts a piece of the Old Country frozen in time, you could say, because their identity was constantly under threat.

That's what employees do when they feel excluded. They protect old habits and resist stepping up or taking risks for the greater good.

Change is the order of the day in the modern economy. It feels like the moment one masters a powerful new technology, they go and change it again! A company that wishes to take advantage of such new developments needs employees who will step up and embrace change for the greater good. In a work environment that leaves employees isolated, that is all but impossible.

The chief ingredient of an inclusive work culture

The foundation for an inclusive work culture is employee

communication. And I'm not talking about email and PowerPoint presentations. An effective employee communications solution provides employees with the information they need to do their job. Beyond stacks of technical manuals they of course will need to use the machinery in their place of work, employees also need:

1. to understand where their contribution fits in the grand scheme of things,
2. to know why the company does things the way it does,
3. a means to contribute their ideas up the food chain to management, and
4. a way to connect on a personal level with fellow employees.

How would you describe your employees' place of work? Is it an embracing culture, or one of isolation? Do you receive new ideas from front line staff, or is the silence deafening?

At PDP we work with companies every day to empower their employees to build an all-inclusive culture. It starts with an authentic, face-to-face conversation with your front line employees, and leads to improved employee retention, employee engagement, and greater productivity.

There really is no downside.

See more at: http://about.pdpsolutions.com/blog/without-effective-employee-communications-employee.shtml

6

Employee Communication: Connected at Home, so why not Connected at Work?

Socially, we live in a highly connected world. We have every piece of information we need. At work, it's often a different story.

FIRST PUBLISHED NOV 3, 2013

Do you know that feeling you get when you forget to take your phone with you? I did that this morning. I dashed from the house to the office and when walking into my office building, I realized I left the darn thing recharging on my kitchen counter. Shoot!

Then I got that unpleasant feeling. I was "unplugged". Panic! I swear, as I processed this fact my steps actually quickened so that I could get to my laptop and log on to my computer ... to be connected again. Whew!

That got me thinking about how accustomed most of us are to being connected all the time. We know what our schedule is, what time it is, what are friends and family are doing, what temperature it is, what is happening in the world and our city – just by looking at our smart phones.

Contrast that to the amount of information employees are provided by their employers. It's likely not real time and comprehensive. So many employees feel "unplugged" – not knowing what is happening in their environment and they have no easy way to tap in to learn more. Employees are somewhat beholden to their companies to get information if and when the company leaders are ready to offer it.

That's quite a different change of pace than what that

little device in our purses or pockets affords us.

Stop making your employees panic in an information void – use PDP's simple tools to open that new line of communication that is regular, disciplined, constructive, fun and measurable.

By the way, I drove back to my house less than an hour in to retrieve my precious phone. i just couldn't stand that feeling of being out of the loop any longer.

To Bold Moves.

See more at: http://about.pdpsolutions.com/blog/employee-communication-connected-at-home-so-why-no.shtml

Employee Disengagement Can Do More Damage Than It's Worth

When it comes to active employee disengagement, a company cannot afford to simply live with it, even to a small degree.

FIRST PUBLISHED NOV 2, 2013

I remember being an executive in a high tech startup some years ago. Out of one hundred employees, even in the best of situations, there was always a small number of employees who just didn't want to work. No one has a 100% hiring success rate, we told ourselves, and with a 95% hiring success rate, we were willing to "leave well enough alone". The problem is, it takes a disproportionate amount of time to manage disengaged employees than it does engaged ones.

In the case of employment, you could say that 20% of employees take 80% of the employee management cycles. Sometimes the problem is, a person is simply a bad fit, and you have to make a graceful parting of company. More often than not, though, it's an issue of engagement. A bad fit can be an easier problem to address because it's usually obvious to everyone and you don't also have to deal with potentially destructive behavior, as you would have to deal with in the case of employee disengagement.

A single disengaged employee can negate the productivity of several of their otherwise productive co-workers.

What we found was, in the high tech startup I mentioned earlier, a disengaged employee could undo the work of a half dozen otherwise engaged employees. That happens in many ways: they simply waste everyone's time talking bad stuff at the water cooler, they infect others with their negative perspectives, and they put people and productivity at risk by their on-the-job behavior. What was thought to be a "5% compromise" in productivity, the company may have actually been losing 25% of what we produced by simply overlooking the less-than-desired results of a few employees.

Still, it's a delicate issue. An employee may be going through a short-lived personal crisis and may appear to be disengaged for a short period of time. I remember being severely jet-lagged in the office a few times and people thought I had lost interest in my work for a few days. I was simply exhausted and confused, as anyone reading this who has experienced continental-level jet-lag will understand. Once my circadian rhythms had re-synchronized, I was fine again. So, you have to also understand enough to see a sustained pattern of disengagement before you tackle a persistent problem head-on. In the meantime, though, there is a phenomenon that provides a return on investment right away. It's called transparency.

Transparency - the panacea

Most companies have something they don't want their competitors to learn about. If it's not the secret formula to a high value brand soft drink like Coca-Cola, it might simply be the details of the company's cost structure. If it were up to me, I would be more interested in my competitor's cost structure than to get access to their software product source code. But I digress.

99% of what's going on in a company is purely operational, and is of little use to competitors. Sometimes, it might even distract and confuse competitors if they were to spend time and money trying to decipher it. And even then, they'd never quite know if what they were reading were in fact true. So I encourage people to contrast the enormous value of front line employees knowing what's going on, why it's going on, and where the company is headed, with the minuscule risk of some competitor discovering and exploiting something valuable. And contrast that too with the risk of a workforce that doesn't know what's going on.

Transparency has almost no downside. Front line employees always do better when they know:
1. Why the company does what it does,
2. Their own place in the grand scheme of things, and
3. Where the company is going.

Those three (let's call them) knowledge points, break out into a lot of operational facts and figures (e.g. how the employee's production division is actually doing). Today, those operational facts are commonly delivered to front line employees via employee information kiosks, a physical element of a complete employee information solution, which I will go into in greater detail in another posting. For today, it is the transparency from such a system that will tackle the issue of the few disengaged employees.

It's almost impossible for a disengaged employee to remain so in an organization committed to transparency. That's because each person's work behavior — management's behavior too, by the way, so be warned — is seen more clearly in such an environment. If an employee remains disengaged, it will be more clearly seen by all for what it is: disengagement, and not some structural or management issue. At that point, an employee has a choice: remain disengaged or join the land of the living, and take advantage of the new employee information solution to get re-engaged! The alternative is to move on to pastures new.

See more at: http://about.pdpsolutions.com/blog/its-easier-to-have-engaged-employees-than-disengag.shtml

The Cookie Thief: Keeping Employees Engaged Means Being Aware Of What They Do For You

It's easy to find fault, but it's far more effective to celebrate all the ways front line employees make the company successful.

FIRST PUBLISHED NOV 1, 2013

There's a poem called The Cookie Thief, recited here by Wayne Dyer you may have heard about. It's about a lady waiting for her plane, accidentally eating half the contents of a pack of cookies belonging to a stranger sitting beside her in an airport departure lounge. She thought she was eating her own cookies, but hers were in fact still in her handbag, she was to discover later. Likely the anecdote is fiction, but the point is, we all are getting something at the expense of someone else. We are usually keenly aware of what we have contributed to others' fortunes, but we don't always have the same sharp eye for what others are doing for us. It's good, therefore, to be on the lookout for ways in which others help us. In fact, it might be safer to assume, and Wayne Dyer would advise us, to work on the assumption someone is making sacrifices on our behalf, and we are simply unaware of it.

Whatever you focus on grows

In the parable of the two wolves, it is the one you feed that determines who you will become.

An Indian Brave was taking counsel from his Tribal Chief one day. He was relating to the Chief how he struggled with the opposing good and evil forces within him, and how he might be tempted to stray from a good path in life. The Chief explained: "inside you there are two wolves. One wolf is of greed, envy, violence, fear and malice. The other wolf is of love, kindness, generosity, forgiveness and charity. They both fight to control who you are." The Indian Brave, puzzled by the story asked "but which one will win, oh honorable Chief?" The Chief smiled and replied softly "the one you feed".

Managing people is like that, insofar as whatever behavior you focus on will grow. We are all like that. Yes, sometimes there are serious issues that need to be dealt with in the work environment, and so, it is not always about slapping each employee on the back to congratulate then for a job well done; there are constructive ways to deal with any difficult issue. Most of the time, though, good behavior will expand to fill the available space if it is focused upon, just as bad behavior will grow if you make that the focus of employee motivation.

It doesn't take much

One aspect of management I didn't get for a long time — and I paid a certain price for that delay — was that employees often hear things a lot louder than you express them. For example, you might say quite casually to front line employees at the water cooler "It's a nice sunny day, today!", thinking it was a harmless greeting and nothing more. Your front line staff, however, could read into it that you were disappointed they were taking too much time at the water cooler and your "greeting" was a veiled reference to how the good weather outside might help them find another job! I'm exaggerating of course, but as a manager, you must claim ownership of the culture and make it one of positive reinforcement, or the vacuum will be filled with guesses and paranoia.

Leave nothing to doubt. Show your gratitude. Even when you're not completely sure of the specifics, you know when your company is doing well, and people on the front line are making that happen.

It's a safe bet that sometime today, you'll be eating from someone else's bag of cookies. I know I will!

See more at: http://about.pdpsolutions.com/blog/the-cookie-thief-keeping-employees-engaged-means-b.shtml

Employee Engagement: Five Reasons To Thank Your Front Line Employees

Put your checkbook away. For full employee engagement, your front line employees are waiting for an honest pat on the back.

FIRST PUBLISHED OCT 31, 2013

This is the second in this seasonal series on the effects of gratitude on employee engagement.

When I was very young — perhaps three or four years old — I used to run into the kitchen from the back yard with worms, insects and other delightful objects I found outside. Each was a gift to my mother, and for each, she would thank me vociferously. I've grown out of that particular behavior, mostly, and my mother doesn't need to pretend anymore that she likes a gift I present to her. Over the years, the worms have been replaced by chocolates, flowers and other gifts. I'm no longer as directly dependent on her as I was five decades ago, but I do understand the impact of any gratitude I show her for the occasional bit of mothering she still affords me. (You know, a home-cooked dinner, a bit of advice about life, types of people to avoid, etc.). It's more of an equal relationship today of course, where the interdependence is more emotional than necessary for survival as it was when I was a child.

Have you thanked a front line employee today? Here are some suggestions on where to start.

It's easy to find fault with one's parents. It's like shooting ducks in a barrel. As a mirror often reflects an opposite image to the viewer, a child can often deliver to its parent the opposite of what a parent sees in the child; a parent sees only goodness and potential in their child, and the child may repay that rose-colored view with cynicism and expressions of dissatisfaction. If you've ever faced the scornful eye of your disgruntled teenage offspring, you'll understand what I mean. It's more like facing a hard-nosed county prosecutor than the loving child who told you a decade earlier I love you daddy. Its basis is in the myriad ways a child takes what they get for granted, and as children, we all did it at least to some degree. Personally, I deal with this dilemma by reminding myself that parenting is not a popularity contest, and that it works itself out in time. The point is, it's easy to take others' service to us for granted.

As adults, even well-adjusted, mature, responsible adults, we still need to be thanked once in a while. So, I got to thinking, what might I, as a manager, be taking for granted that my employees are doing for me or the company we all work for? Many work environments don't readily present an obvious list, so I made up a list of my own. I've made it as general as possible, with a few specific ones too, so you might be able to cherry-pick a few to use with your own front line employees:

Thank you for working directly with our customers every day. I don't hear about every customer interaction, but I know that you deal with challenges there every day, and it is perhaps because I don't hear much, you're handling things well for us.

1. Thanks for being patient with the management team. We probably don't check in with you often enough, but we do recognize and appreciate that you and your team is keeping the front lines of this company operational every day.
2. Thanks to you and your colleagues for keeping this environment an accident-free zone for so long. We understand it takes a little longer to get things done the safe way, but we also know it affects the company's bottom line positively. We appreciate that.
3. Thanks for introducing your friend Jimmy to the company, and for helping get him up-to-speed on what we do here and his on-the-job training. Intro-

ductions like that make my life easier and show us the level of dedication you clearly have for our company.
4. I looked at the productivity numbers yesterday, and I see your team has achieved the best month's productivity in six months, and the lowest defects-per-thousand across all of our production units.

As you can see, it's pretty easy to find reasons to thank your front line employees. And you can turn good news into better news simply by drawing attention to positive behavior.

It's easy to take for granted what employees do for you. It's easy to say it's what we're paying them to do, but it will actually cost you nothing to reach out and give them a pat on the back. It's what they're waiting for.

See more at: http://about.pdpsolutions.com/blog/employee-engagement-five-reasons-to-thank-your-fro.shtml

Gratitude: The Quickest Path to Full Employee Engagement
An effective and immediate result of gratitude is increased employee engagement.

FIRST PUBLISHED OCT 30, 2013

I find it easy enough to write every day about internal communication and employee engagement. I've been an employee for more than half of my working life, and have always been serving clients no matter what I did for a living. If you think about, Bob Dylan was right when he said Gotta Serve Somebody. Really, the only question that remains is, will you do it willingly or unwillingly. Whichever choice you make will have a profound impact on the quality of your work — and the people you serve — so let's examine what employees need so that they serve willingly.

Over the decades I have worked, salary was more of a "checkbox item" than a motivator. I remember one of the final interviews I had with a big software company a couple of decades ago; the hiring manager asked me what salary I was expecting. Being my first job in the United States, I really had no clue what a good salary was, and I wasn't expecting the question. I simply replied the right one. It's the kind of answer that can derail an interview, but in my case, it worked very well. I simply wasn't that interested in salary; I felt they could tell me what the salary was and we'd just get on with it. I was more interested in the company itself, their exciting products, and of course, emigrating to the United States. What's more, I don't even remember what my salary was. But I do remember the many occasions where managers were grateful for the work I did. To me, a little bit of recognition gave me a far better handle on what my future was than any salary did.

Gratitude, some say, is the most powerful force in the universe.

Reaching out to employees

The challenge with showing gratitude is this: you had better mean it. Employees know the difference between authentic gratitude for the work they've done, and the false praise that is often delivered to them as a means of manipulation. People know if you care or not. The way I've always got in tune with my own gratitude for employees is to remind myself of the time and effort they put into the company I have a stake in. Most employers are beholden to their employees for the trust they put into that employer's hands.

The moment an employee takes a new position, they take a risk. Will the new employer deliver on their promises? How will this new position help me grow my career? Is the culture conducive to getting engaged and motivated? The trust they have in you as an employer is the first reason to thank them.

When you take that first step on your path of gratitude for the work your front line employees do, leave your mobile phone behind in your office. Give that outreach 100% of your attention, as you go on your first real journey of MBWA (Management By Walking Around). You might do a little research on the few employees you intend to thank today, by looking at their recent work record. Perhaps an email came from a customer, or a production record was surpassed. A particular achievement might have been a team effort, in which case, you now have the opportunity to meet each team member to thank them personally.

Whatever the reason for the gratitude, consider expressing it today. It's possibly the single most effective — costing nothing, essentially — way to get your employees re-engaged.

See more at: http://about.pdpsolutions.com/blog/gratitude-the-quickest-path-to-full-employee-engag.shtml

11

Employee Engagement is Required to Build Today's Complex Products

Thousands of workers can be involved in the creation of 21st century quality products. And that only works when they are fully engaged.

FIRST PUBLISHED OCT 29, 2013

There is a Chinese proverb that goes Tell me and I'll forget; show me and I may remember; involve me and I'll understand.

Today's manufacturing unit is far more complex than it was a generation ago. The reason is simple: new technology has allowed extraordinary advances in product and service quality. Everything from super jumbo aircraft to automobiles to telephones have all experienced explosive improvements in quality, reliability and safety.

Times have changed: In the 1960s, the typical family car would be lucky to run for 100,000 miles. It would break down perhaps once a year and many were death traps.

I've read that you would have to board an airplane forty million times to have a 50:50 chance of dying as a result of an air crash. Motor cars manufactured today can be expected to run for 200,000 to 300,000 miles before they are discarded. In the 1960s, a car would be on its last proverbial legs by the time it passed 100,000 miles. What's really surprising is, they are far more complex machines today than they were back then. My parents' 1960 Ford Anglia station wagon, broke down approximately once a year, and it happened with pretty much all cars of the time.

With complexity comes dependency

When the Wright Brothers' primitive plane first left the ground, two or three people were involved in that first test flight. When the Boeing 787 took its first test flight, there were thousands of people involved, not just the small number of flight engineers on board. Those thousands of employees made it possible to do this extraordinary feat, as long as they were in excellent communication with one another. As technology advances further — as it surely will — a manufacturer becomes more and more dependent upon the individuals that make up the team. They deliver an ever more complex service to their employer, working with increasingly complex tools. It's no longer sufficient to bellow commands down the corridors of one's business and expect work to be done. Today, employees from the front lines of the company have a profound influence — for good or bad — over the product and service quality of their employers. This means they have to be fully engaged at every step of the way.

What is it like in your company? Do you feel like the products and services your company provides are 21st century quality? Do your products run for 300,000 miles, or do they fall apart long before their time? It might be time to get your employees engaged. It all starts with you and them talking with one another. We can help you with that first step with a simple phone call.

See more at: http://about.pdpsolutions.com/blog/employee-engagement-is-required-to-build-todays-co.shtml

12

The Dichotomy—or "Catch 22"—of Poor Internal Communication

Internal communication problems present a unique challenge to management. It's hard to solve the problem with the very tools you need to solve it.

FIRST PUBLISHED OCT 28, 2013

Having a serious internal communications problem is like clinical depression or the need for a bank loan, in this respect at least: the very condition impedes the organization's (or person's) ability to solve the problem itself. It deprives the organization of an effective solution: internal communication. If the company has an issue with its power supply, vendor selection, wifi configuration or invoicing software, it can use its internal communication system to help solve the problem. Not so, however, when the company is suffering from poor internal communication, because it doesn't have it to solve it.

You've probably applied for credit at some point where the lending institution's reply was something like come back to us when you don't need it.

An internal communications problem is a Catch 22 situation: You need it to solve it.

In the famous novel Catch 22, the eponymous principle was that you would have to be crazy to fly, but if you were crazy, you would be grounded. If you were grounded because you feared the real dangers of flying, it would be proof that you were sane, so you could fly, etc., etc.. It was from that "double bind", or circular logic, that the term Catch 22 entered common use in the English language.

A serious internal communication problem presents a dichotomy to the organization, because you need to communicate together in order to come up with a plan to solve the problem. If you can do that, it could be argued, you don't have an internal communication problem. This is the central reason why getting an internal communications initiative underway is, to a degree, half the battle. And it's why we encourage prospective clients to include front line staff from the very beginning, including the first demonstration of the PDP solution.

By the time a prospect makes their first call to us, a lot has already happened. They have acknowledged that there is a problem, and have taken the first steps towards solving it. If fact, it is our prospects who have educated us about what the requirement is. By the time we hear their voice in the first online demonstration, we simply focus on how well the PDP solution matches their needs, and we spend little or no time describing the need for internal communications solution in general.

There is a common theme among successful initiatives to solve an internal communications problem. It is to reach outside the organization in order to get the solution moving. At PDP, we help organizations with that first step, getting things moving and keeping them moving. Even if you are struggling internally to get the ball rolling, give us a call. We can help.

See more at: http://about.pdpsolutions.com/blog/engaging-employees-is-the-only-way-theyll-ever-und.shtml

13

Making Employee Communication More Effective, Transparent and Fun

Out with the cork boards, in with interactive touch screens. Employee communication arrives in the 21st century.

FIRST PUBLISHED OCT 27, 2013

If you've ever felt overwhelmed with technology, I sympathize. Within a single day, you might come in contact with a TV remote control, a smartphone, iPad, laptop, desk computer, a GPS system, an ATM, a high tech oven, a color printer and countless other gadgets. And just as you get to master one of these pieces of technology, they introduce a replacement for it. Your learning curve, it seems, has become a permanent uphill climb.

When technology first emerges, it can be a little rough

My parents had the same telephone for my entire childhood. We had that phone, a TV set and a radio, and each of these simple pieces of equipment was taken care of.

I've noticed something else that has been happening lately. People under twenty-five years of age seem to have an innate ability to decode acronyms. Their generation has been using a type of shorthand in handheld devices so much, this acronym deciphering skill grew from it. Is there no end to the growing complexity of our lives!

It has to be fun

When technologies are first introduced, they can be a bit rough. The first real mobile phone would tire your arm out after a few minutes holding it to your ear. When the man played by actor Michael Douglas was released from prison, he collected the cellphone they kept for him while he was imprisoned. I remember in the theater at the time I watched the movie, everyone laughing at how large the phone was compared to the phones people were using just a few years later.

We don't call them mobile phones or cell phones now. We call them smart phones. That's because the average such phone today has more computer power than NASA Mission Control had during the Apollo Moon landings.

Powerful and all as they are, not everything that's smart is good. Personally, I have gotten more selective about the technology I let into my life. It's no longer good enough to be functional. I like it to be fun, too.

What struck me about one of our valued clients today was how he described the PDP system as being fun. For him, it wasn't just about the business purpose of the solution. Because they included personal stories and information in the PDP solution, people were more drawn into it. Even though he could use his desk computer to access the DP information system, he often preferred to use the shop floor-based PDP touch-screen to catch up on the latest news. He said it was more fun to do it that way, and put him directly in touch with front line staff in a way he would not be otherwise.

Take a look at this very short video snippet to see what I mean. If you're not convinced, give us a call and we'll show you how much fun it can be.

See more at: http://about.pdpsolutions.com/blog/making-employee-communication-more-effective-trans.shtml

14

Employee Communications: The What, the How and the Why

In a nutshell, why no company should be without an employee communications solution, what it is, and how it's put together.

FIRST PUBLISHED OCT 26, 2013

I often get asked, What is it all about, the PDP solution?

The What— In the simplest terms, PDP delivers a means and method for increasing the level of communication between the leadership team of a company, and its front line staff. It enables a flow of information from the "top" of the organization to the people who are making it happen: the front line staff. It also monitors the "read" rate of transmission, so it's also understood the degree to which the message is being received by the front line staff. It's also bi-directional. Communication back from front line staff to management is facilitated, ensuring the flow of new ideas and intelligence on what is happening on the front lines of the company.

The How— An effective employee communication solution will typically include employee information kiosks using touch-screen technology, specifically designed to support the industry they are used in. Software will connect the system to corporate assets and databases, and non-desk employees (those who do not have on-the-job access to email and personal computers) will be able to log in at a location close to where they work, either to read transmitted information, to make inquiries, or to input specific data. Wifi is often used, and the system is secured and/or encrypted for two-way transmissions.

The Why— Studies have shown that engaged employees drive up productivity. And the simplest, most effective way to improve employee engagement is to connect management and front line employees in four ways: (1) Messaging from leadership to front line staff (2) transparency into how messages are being received (3) access to work-related, information for front line staff, and (4) ideas and feedback from front line staff to management. An employee communications solution will provide all four channels, and in a way that is secure, tailored and satisfies all four channels.

See more at: http://about.pdpsolutions.com/blog/employee-communications-the-what-the-how-and-the-w.shtml

Employee Communications: Transparency Every Company Should Have

An acquisition is hard to imagine for a company that doesn't offer the transparency of an internal communications solution.

FIRST PUBLISHED OCT 25, 2013

Fifty years ago, a telephone company might have gotten away with lack of transparency. Not any more!

As a child growing up, I lived in a time when a telephone bill had two numbers on it. One was your telephone number and the other was how much you owed the telephone company. The one telephone company was state-run and it was a monopoly. You either paid your bill or you got cut off. There was no way to verify which calls made up the charge, and it was all done on faith. I often wondered how they actually calculated the numbers, with the types of equipment they must have been using behind the scenes. It was all a big secret and ... well ... the telephone company was the staple of jokes everywhere.

Today, no one would tolerate such a situation, or so we would believe. Imagine being able to send an invoice to customers without any transparency into what it was made up of. But, guess what. It still happens in a different way today. In corporate acquisitions everywhere, there is scant attention paid to what's happening between management and employees during a due diligence[1] process. The books are pored over, products are examined for quality, markets are studied and funnels are measured. People know that the connection between front line staff and the leadership team is critical, but there's usually no way to determine what kind of shape it's in. It's taken on faith, and the value of the would-be transaction is discounted while that uncertainty exists.

What if there was a way to determine the health of relationships and communication between front line staff and the leadership team? What if potential investors, clients or business partners had a way to see what kind of shape the company was in when it came to employee engagement? Well, there is. It's called an Internal Communications Solution — a.k.a. an Employee Communications Solution — and it provides direct insight into how front line staff is communicating back to the management team. It also monitors the "read" rate of information pushed from the management team to the front line. And that's not even counting the hugely beneficial effects on employee engagement.

Considering the profound effect an effective internal communications solution can have on the productivity of a company, it's hard to imagine making an acquisition offer for a company that has none. An internal communications solution today will be considered a necessity tomorrow. Just like safety belts and airbags forty years and twenty years ago, respectively, we'll all wonder how on Earth we survived without them for so long.

An effective internal communications solution increases (1) the value of a company, (2) its chances of being acquired, (3) its likelihood of investment and (4) productivity. There's really no downside.

[1]*Due diligence is the examination of a company and its circumstances before an investment or acquisition is initiated.*

See more at: http://about.pdpsolutions.com/blog/employee-communications-transparency-every-company.shtml

Making Changes for Improved Employee Engagement

Sharing information can be disruptive, but the new transparency often inspires front line staff to perform at their best levels.

FIRST PUBLISHED OCT 24, 2013

I have taken quite a hiatus from offering any of my own entries for this Blog. It has been a busy couple of weeks having taken PDP on the road to several conferences. We have gotten very favorable feedback and heard some interesting insights about what is and is not going on in the world of employee communications. I will write up some thoughts in upcoming posts!

From one-way to two-way

For now, I share a comparison that came to mind while driving last month here in my city. When we moved here years ago all the streets were two-way. Over time, they switched to mostly one-way; roads that were in place for decades. Then recently with thoughts of city revitalization, especially in the city center, the streets were converted back to two-way.

After driving them for so long, I feared I would mess up on the two ways and get into an accident. I was convinced it was a bad idea and that I was going to hate having this two-way business to deal with.

I was wrong.

Actually, it all worked out very well and it is now much easier to get around town. I have witnessed only a few minor fender benders by unfortunate drivers who also had to take it a little slower – and look both ways instead of one. The new routes have actually made it easier to move about town. I like it!

I admit, if I had had my druthers, I would have voted to leave it as is. Isn't that also the case with sharing information in our companies? It is easier to just "do it the way we have always done it."

From one-way communication to two-way communication

I am reminded of one of our clients that decided to start sharing a key performance metric with their entire organization. The metric is Dollars Shipped. The CEO will tell you that when she first proposed publishing this metric using PDP's Score feature, there was some resistance from people in the front office who could not understand why you would want to do that. There was fear that if the front line staff were to see actual dollar figures for how much the product cost — product that was shipping from their location every day — they would be shocked and would become disenchanted.

What happened was the exact opposite. The staff rallied, remembering the benchmarks they had hit in years past. They wanted to once again hit those marks and worked harder to achieve it. Sharing that information engaged employees and motivated them in a new way.

It takes courage to change — especially when it comes to sharing information — to do something new and unfamiliar, forcing you to change your habits. Nevertheless, it can be worth it!

See more at: http://about.pdpsolutions.com/blog/making-changes-for-the-better.shtml

Internal Communications: Nature Always Wins

When it comes to internal communications solutions, mother knows best. Person-to-person communication is pivotal to success.

FIRST PUBLISHED OCT 23, 2013

Fads come and go, trendy fashions repeat in cycles, and we are always living in one New Age or another. It seems as if, as the saying goes, the more things change, the more they stay the same. The one constant you can rely upon, as my mother often reminds me, is that Nature always has the last word.

My career is long enough to have covered (in approximate order of appearance) mainframes, mini-computers,

ATMs, personal computers, laptops, email, the Internet, cell phones, Wifi, and now we have smartphones, the Cloud, touch-screens and Tablets. Each came with great promise, each delivered much, and there is surely more to come.

Despite incredible technology at our fingertips, person-to-person communication will always play a pivotal role in successful internal communications.

Still, there's nothing like face-to-face contact with real human beings to keep one sane. That's because we've been creatures who solved problems face-to-face for a million years, and have been using technology for only a few generations. We are wired to be with each other, in close physical proximity.

We humans communicate not just with words, of course, but in other non-verbal ways, some of which we barely understand. It means that, while technology is immensely powerful, person-to-person communication will never go away completely. It's part of the mix of every effective internal communication solution. It's why we recommend, especially at the outset of an internal communications solution implementation, a generous helping of MBWA (Management By Walking Around). The CEO or General Manager will come face-to-face with front line staff, and front line staff will absorb his or her message far more effectively. So while the technology aspects of your new internal communications solution are essential, the personal touch is also indispensable. My apologies to all those hermits out there who prefer never to leave their office.

If face-to-face didn't count for anything, the President would never have to leave the White House. The presence of a leader on the shop floor has a disproportionate influence over what happens. It's why business leaders jet across the world for a thirty-minute, face-to-face meeting with partners of colleagues. It's just very hard to do business without it.

Internal Communications solutions usually have a technology component to them. Typically they will have touch-screen employee information kiosks, custom software, an interface to the company's existing databases, processes and key contributors. With all that high tech power, the human element is still indispensable. Person-to-person communication is integral to the very first steps of your internal communications solution, and it is involved in every single step thereafter. We know from experience that the personal involvement of the leadership team at the beginning is a huge predictor of future levels of success.

Perhaps that is nothing surprising, really. We humans have had a million years to get the hang of it.

See more at: http://about.pdpsolutions.com/blog/internal-communications-nature-always-wins.shtml

Internal Communication: Getting a Company Into Ship Shape Opens Interesting Doors

Internal communication increases transparency, opening doors to outside strategic opportunity, customer favor, and investor interest.

FIRST PUBLISHED OCT 22, 2013

A for-profit business, by definition, is a machine for generating wealth. There is investment, and there are expectations of future returns on that investment. Some elements of the investment are to increase return, and other elements are meant to minimize risk to securing that return. For example, adding a new smelting furnace might be a way to increase the capacity to support growing revenue and profit; hiring a safety professional might an investment to reduce the risk of catastrophic liability claims.

An investment in an internal communications solution satisfies both growth of income potential and the reduction of risk. The transparency it brings to the company makes it easier for outside parties — at the discretion of the organization's leadership, of course — to examine the true value of the company, without having to guess or live with additional elements of uncertainty.

The transparency delivered by an internal communications solution shows that a company has nothing to hide. Especially from itself.

I'll come back to that point in a moment. First I want to relate to you something I learned about venture capital funding, how investors look at potential investment opportunities, and causation versus correlation.

It is often said in the venture capital community that companies are more likely to reach a liquidity event if they have received venture capital investment in the past. I don't dispute that assertion, but I will ask you the chicken-or-the-egg question: Does venture capital investment increase the chances of success for the company they invest in, or do venture capital companies simply ride companies which were heading for glory to begin with?

As a rule-of-thumb, I would recommend any high-tech startup to go through the process of seeking venture capital funding, but then to decline the offer unless (a) it is simply the only way to pay for things they absolutely need to be successful or (2) you the owner don't believe the company will be successful and therefore wish to sell some stock now while you can. (I am sorry if that sounds cynical. Don't worry about venture capitalists; they will look after themselves.) I recommend to go through the so-called due-diligence process with the VCs simply because they will force you to be transparent in all or most of your important business processes. That achievement alone increases your chances of success because it brings to light issues lurking in the shadows of your company. And to receive what they call a "term sheet" (an offer of investment in your company) VCS will need to see many things in place. Mostly, such things are commonly known indicators of success — and axiomatically, fewer warning signs — that venture capital investment experts know from experience and education to be generally true.

How does this relate to Internal Communication?

An internal communications system brings to light issues lurking in the shadows of your company, just as preparation for a potential investment does. It also brings great ideas to the surface, but from a potential investor's point of view, the transparency allows a VC to evaluate your company as a possible investment opportunity, if that is of interest to your company leadership. It's like a health check of sorts. Knowing what is going on is always better than not knowing what is going on. It is why, when managers or employees have direct experience of a modern internal communications solution, they find it hard to ever again work without one.

Internal communication, in apparent contradiction to its name, is also about what goes on outside the company. Investors, partners and customers all look more favorably on a company that embraces the process of internal communication. Instinctively, they know you will make a more dependable partner, all else being equal. It's the investment with no downside, and once you've tried it, there's no going back to the old stuff.

See more at: http://about.pdpsolutions.com/blog/internal-communication-getting-a-company-into-ship.shtml

Employee Engagement: Soliciting the Help of Goats

Today's article is on effective ways to get your internal communication and employee engagement initiative underway.

FIRST PUBLISHED OCT 21, 2013

I was reading recently about a small business in Seattle that employs goats to do the company's work. People needing a patch of land cleared can opt to rent the services of a dozen hungry goats. A truck carrying twelve of the eager little workers would show up, the driver (himself a human, not a goat, of course) would lead the hungry animals onto the piece of land and, tethered to a specific area of the land, all twelve goats would proceed to eat everything down to its roots. Within a few days, the hitherto densely overgrown patch of land was cleared and ready for repurposing. (I hear they have since added an additional service: hungry pigs who would follow the goats and churn up the soil for agricultural use).

Years ago where I grew up in Dublin, Ireland, I read of

a man who would buy an overgrown property for a fraction of its real value, so cheap because in many cases the house was inaccessible due to the density of brambles and out of control bushes or trees all around it. He was buying $100,000 houses (that was a lot in those days) for less than half their potential value. He would tether a few goats to the house, giving them enough line to reach everything growing around the house. the goats would eat and eat, seemingly day and night, until the house was cleared. It became such a phenomenon, national TV showed a time-lapse clearing of one of his projects. The goats did such a thorough and fine job, the house and its grounds were easy to resurrect once the goats had done their bit. A modest investment in decoration and basic landscaping would see the house back on the market at an attractive profit.

Clearing out all the weeds and overgrowth added immediate value to the original investment.

More companies than not are more like one of those houses covered in brambles, inaccessible and largely uninhabitable. The lack of transparency, and of internal communications, makes the business difficult to manage, less profitable and of less value. The return on investment into an internal communications solution is so overwhelming, and the path to success so clear, it might be the single most predictable way to increase the value of a business.

A whole industry has grown up around the science and art of improved employee engagement. People are choosing the subject as a career choice for life. It's because companies are reaching out for help, and services are emerging as a result of that demand. It's a way of protecting valuable assets. Companies spend so much on hiring the best talent they can afford, yet neglect the the optimization of what that investment brings to their company.

Perhaps the most common obstacle companies face is knowing where to start. By the time most companies reach out to us for help, they have a solid understanding of what they are trying to achieve, but are unsure of where to start. Call us today. We can help you take the first steps.

See more at: http://about.pdpsolutions.com/blog/employee-engagement-soliciting-the-help-of-goats.shtml

Employee Engagement. It's What People Do All Day

Engaged employees are the only kind you ever want. And it's what employees want too, because it means that every day feels like Saturday.

FIRST PUBLISHED OCT 20, 2013

" Only ten percent of employees are engaged", (Source:
Engage for Success, the MacLeod Report). Say it ain't so. Having been an employee for half of my career, I can only feel sorry for the 90% of people who arrive at work disengaged. The day must be long indeed.

Let's look at two consequences of the alarming statistic; one bad, the other good, but first, you might enjoy this entertaining video on the subject of what is means to be engaged, both for the employee and the employe

Keeping employees engaged, to many, sounds sometimes like managing children. That's why people shy away from it. They don't want to seem like they are subject to the very human characteristic of needing a little encouragement. In reality, even — and perhaps especially — the people at the top of the organization need a little encouragement, respect and recognition for a job well done.

When employees are actively engaged — and I speak from my own experience here, having lived on both sides of the engagement divide — they live healthier lives, both at home and at work. I know when I am engaged in my work, I sleep better, so much the more prepared to jump out of bed in the morning to tackle another great day in paradise. I would go so far as to say that every day is Saturday when you are engaged in your work.

When an employee is engaged in the work they do, their productivity flows from the inside of them. They don't have to torture the work out of themselves. And here's another funny (and sad in another way) short video representation of someone leaving work (the penguin) on a Friday, and another going to work on Monday morning (the polar bear).

Which kind of employees would you prefer?

Call us today for a thirty-minute demonstration on how we help our clients turn their organization into an engaged-only team of highly productive penguins ... ahem ... I mean, employees!

See more at: http://about.pdpsolutions.com/blog/employee-engagement-its-what-people-do-all-day.shtml

21

Internal Communication and the Daily Act of Brushing One's Teeth

Why internal communication is not something you set and leave alone. It's a few simple habits. Then it's easy.

FIRST PUBLISHED OCT 19, 2013

Years ago I had a neighbor who would, every year at the height of spring, buy a complete set of weed-whackers and related equipment, then attack his overgrown yard with all the new found energy of a young bull. He would exhaust himself over a single weekend bringing the job to 90% completion, then abandon the project, leaving the new equipment where it fell, exposed then to the elements for twelve months. Come mid-spring of the following year, he would toss the weather-destroyed equipment out with the trash, buy another new set, and waste himself over another weekend, repeating this cycle year after year. It was the crash diet of yard work, you could say, taken to a pathological level.

My neighbor did know what had to be done. All he needed to do was a little bit every day, and not destroy himself in one burst of energy over a single weekend. His problem was, he never developed a simple habit of a little a day.

What!! Did the teacher just say something interesting?

Decades ago, a teacher of mine made a lasting impression on me with some advice he delivered. (It was on one of a handful of moments I was actually paying attention to any of my teachers). He said any student in the class could increase his effective IQ by ten percentage points by doing one thing: forming good habits. He followed that with another assertion, that for another ten IQ points, a student simply had to get organized. The successful people in the classroom, he said, were not the academically brightest, but rather, that small handful who would follow his two suggestions. He mentioned a few everyday examples: flossing regularly, going to bed on time, and always aiming to arrive at appointments ten minutes early, as ways to improve one's life and prospects significantly over the long term.

Implementing an internal communications — often called employee communications — solution is a bit like managing a nice yard. You just have to do a little every day and the task will all but take care of itself. If your internal communication is out of control today, you might need a little extra attention up-front, but it's easy after that.

When I lived in that house I mentioned earlier, here in the Pacific Northwest, every day I came home, as I walked through my own front yard, I would pull out a few weeds or prune back a shrub here or there. The yard always looked nice and it never got to the point where it needed remedial action. True, to get the nice yard in the first place, I put a little more work in, but once in place, it was easy to maintain. I just had to get into the habit of it. What made the habit easy was the commitment to doing at least something, however small, every time I set foot in the yard.

Effective internal communications work on the same principle. Every time you walk past, you must chip in a little. Once you've established that habit, it becomes easy, and it will pay dividends over and over. In fact, it will be the easiest thing you do all day. It might be simply to walk across the factory floor on your way to your back office, stopping to check in with at least one front line staff member each time, instead of taking the more secluded route from the parking lot where you would meet no one.

And just like my neighbor with the weekend burst of energy, certainly good tools are essential to getting the process moving. Once up and running, though, a little maintenance is all that's required, both for the tools and the processes. And that's all that habits really are: processes.

What about your place of work? Do you feel like it's a bit out of control communication-wise? We can help you take the first few steps in getting your internal communication solution into place. We will also give you the tools and processes you need to keep it in ship shape with very little ongoing effort. It is how we help our clients every day. Are you ready for a thirty-minute online demonstration? Call us today.

See more at: http://about.pdpsolutions.com/blog/internal-communication-and-the-daily-act-of-brushi.shtml

Internal Communications: From The Top, Down or From The Bottom, Up?

Your internal communications initiative will begin at the top, and front line staff will play a central role, if it is to be successful.

FIRST PUBLISHED OCT 18, 2013

When I began as a computer programmer many years ago, there was a witty cartoon floating around with a manager instructing a room full of computer programmers. He said "you start coding. I'll go find out what they want." Funny as it was, it resonates to this day because it happens in real life. The very human principle plays out not just with computer programmers and their managers, but in every part of a company. It's human nature to believe that people just know what to do, so front line staff more often than not, get left to their devices. Over time, they solve problems their own way, and guess at what the company might want or where it is going.

You can't get wet from the word water

Every internal communications initiative will begin at the top of the organization and will involve front line staff as early as possible.

Just as front line employees do not get the benefit of management's direction, organization leadership can miss out on valuable insights that can only come from front line staff. Just think, every moment you spend perfecting that PowerPoint presentation, your front line staff get more experience of what is happening in ... well ... the real world. In the world of commerce, it is like combat experience. There is no substitute for the experience, and it's where all the best ideas are born.

For organizational leadership to be effective, it must be connected with front line staff. If it is not, new solutions, initiatives and plans risk being out of touch with reality, and falling far short of what your customers, employees and shareholders need to be effective.

Imagine not being able to swim. Instead of taking swimming lessons, you read Swimming for Dummies cover to cover, then jump in the deep end of a swimming pool. (Warning: do not do this in real life. I only use it as a hypothetical example). That is how out of touch many companies' leaders become. They have a theoretical understanding — and sometimes not even that — of how their company is connecting with the real world, but they have not internalized it. Meeting your front line staff face-to-face is the first important step in any internal communications initiative. It is because, you can't get wet from the word water.

It all comes from the top

If you are waiting for your front line staff to get the internal communications ball rolling you will likely be disappointed. Remember, you are the boss. It's why they call the top of the org chart the organization's leadership. You might have the occasional extremely proactive front line employee who will spearhead his or her own initiative — perhaps from the benefit of a previous job — but most if not all will await your instructions. It must come from the top.

The message comes from the top: This organization is committed to internal communication. It's a big message to communicate because you're doing it precisely because you need to improve communication. It comes from the top, but must have serious buy-in from front line staff. It's why at PDP we encourage prospects' employees to get involved from the very first software demonstration. The sooner they are involved, the better the results will be.

See more at: http://about.pdpsolutions.com/blog/internal-communications-from-the-top-down-or-from-.shtml

23

The Lack of Internal Communications is Reason #3 Why Companies Make Poor Products

The bigger a company is, the less willing they are to communicate internally. Their strength becomes their weakness.

FIRST PUBLISHED OCT 17, 2013

Have you ever worked in a company where the communication between Marketing and Product Management was less than optimal? Let me ask the question another way. Have you ever worked in a company where communication between those two groups was good? According to this tongue-in-cheek (and be warned, a little profane) article on the online Cracked magazine, it's Reason Number 3 behind the creation of poor products. Most companies struggle to keep that communication working. Perhaps it's because of that, any company who can address the issue even partially has a chance to get ahead of the game.

In the land of the blind, the one-eyed man is king

Small companies compete with big companies by preying on big companies' inherent weakness: a reduced ability to communicate internally.

Anyone who has worked in a large corporation — and any of those with half an eye in their head — has a sense of the difficulties of internal communications. Heck, most couples struggle with it. Imagine trying to get 50,000 employees to communicate effectively with each other! Still, some companies do manage it. They refuse to accept the business as usual mantra of large, stagnant companies, and reach for a better reality. Those companies understand where their success story begins: Internal Communication. They know it's a tough nut to crack, and for that very reason, it will help them get ahead of the crowd.

How small companies beat big companies

I've always been fascinated by how small companies compete. To the uninitiated, a big company should always prevail in any given market, you would think. But if you look at what actually happens, it's often not the case. The reason is, bigger companies tend to be involved in more activities and more markets, and because of that, they run into conflicts with their own interests. For example, the hugely successful Microsoft corporation could not do what it needed to do in the mobile phone space, because they were more interested in bolstering their ownership of the desktop market. As a result, competitors were able to focus — without compromise — on truly solving the customer problem, and muscle into markets owned my Microsoft.

Smaller companies have fewer interests, and are therefore more able to deal with an issue head-on. Still, it doesn't happen automatically. For product management to identify the optimal mix of product growth and time-to-market, it must have a clear understanding of what features and benefits can be sold, juxtaposed with what it costs in engineering terms to deliver them. A product-oriented company that masters that mix has a huge advantage, and it depends more on internal communication than anything else. Improving internal communication in a small company is easier than doing it in a large company. That's one way small companies beat big companies.

Effective, long term threats from small companies creep up on big companies slowly. They move in on a piece of a market slowly enough that the owners of that market don't always recognize the threat until it is too late. And even if the would-be dominant player does see the threat, they are often powerless to respond effectively. Their own internal conflicts impede them just enough for the smaller player to gain a defensible foothold for long enough to ultimately own it. The initially dominant player is beaten by the smaller company with fewer resources. But it only works when the smaller player masters their own internal communication.

See more at: http://about.pdpsolutions.com/blog/the-lack-of-internal-communications-is-reason-3-wh.shtml

Employee Engagement: Can't I Just Let My Supervisors Handle It?
The job of the chief executive is to defend and protect the cultural values of the organization.

FIRST PUBLISHED OCT 16, 2013

I often get the question how does owning one's culture affect employee engagement? I'll get to the answer further down, but first, I want to give a bit of background.

Anyone who has built a company from scratch knows how doubling the number of employees does not automatically mean doubling productivity. In fact, once you move beyond one person — you — to taking on your first employee, perhaps in the form of a business partner, you know there is ramp-up time to consider. In addition, going forward, merely communicating with your new employee takes at least some time. And communicate you must. How else are they going to learn the job, why they are there, and what you expect of them?

There's no better alternative to delivering the corporate message than from the very top of the organization.

In one company I co-founded years ago, I uncovered an assumption I had been making for years up to that point. I had assumed everyone knew what we were all about. Wasn't it obvious! Well, it wasn't obvious. It's always obvious to the visionary, which is why they often omit to share that big vision with everyone else. And that is often the problem with leaders or visionaries in an organization. They themselves have known for so long the why behind everything that goes on that they think it's either obvious, or someone would have naturally brought everyone up-to-date. In reality, people on the ground floor are usually left in the dark.

Sharing is caring

We know taking on employees is a big responsibility. As an employer, you might have many employees, while each employee — typically — has but the one employer. They have, so to speak, all their eggs in one basket; all their hopes are pinned on the one source of income, prosperity and career. Knowing versus not knowing, for the typical employee, is the difference between success and failure. When you share with them information your front line employees need to do their job, you not only improve the productivity of your company, you improve the lives of your employees in many different ways. And the first thing every employee needs to know is their employer's cultural values.

People know who's in charge, so it has to come from the top

Clearly, supervisors and all levels of manager will communicate up and down and across the organization on a daily or moment-by-money basis. When it comes to cultural values, though, the message must always come from — or be understood to come from — the chief executive. Cultural values are like a "constitution" of a company. (I can see the emails coming to me now from legal scholars. I welcome them!) When a president — the Commander-in-Chief, remember — is being inaugurated, the first thing they ask him or her (yes, that's coming) to do is to swear to protect the Constitution. No surprise there.

Owning your culture is protecting your constitution

When I first joined the PDP team, I didn't fully understand the meaning of owning one's culture. That is, the culture within the organization the leaders are responsible for. As I studied the principles behind it, though, it became clearer to me how significant it is. Without a Constitution, the spirit of a nation can be hijacked by special interests, outside forces or nefarious individuals. Knowing the values are held sacred at the very top means every citizen knows where they fit, what their purpose is, and where the organization is going. When that Constitution is threatened, it becomes difficult to work for the greater good.

It's the same with companies. When employees know that the company's culture values — its Constitution — are being protected and owned by the leadership, it's easier to work for the greater good. It's because each employee now has a compass with which to measure their own contribution. They know right from wrong, and good from bad, so it is known what behavior is acceptable. When the cultural values are not understood, that's when disengagement sets it. The corporate equivalent of street gangs step in to fill the void.

Owning your culture is about internal communication. It's the day-to-day reiteration of the organization's cultural values. It must pervade every message coming from anyone in a leadership position. It keeps employees engaged and everyone pointing in the same direction. And the result is always the same: Greater productivity.

See more at: http://about.pdpsolutions.com/blog/employee-engagement-cant-i-just-let-my-supervisors.shtml

Employee Engagement: The Good, the Bad and the Ugly

A company with even a so-so employee engagement level can outpace a poor one's profits by three or four times.

FIRST PUBLISHED OCT 15, 2013

This is my second in a series on the productivity gains available to those companies who improve their employee engagement rates by implementing an effective internal communications solution. Today, I'm quoting some numbers worked out by my favorite research group, the Gallup Organization. I've come to respect their findings, even when what they deliver is a hard pill to swallow.

In a recent article in their Business Journal, they drew a stark comparison between the profitability of companies with a 75% employee engagement rate (the "Good") and companies with a 50% engagement rate (the "Ugly"). That is, organizations where engaged employees outnumber disengaged employees three to one, and organizations that had one disengaged employee for every engaged employee. The former "saw 2.6 times more growth in earnings per share" than the latter.

Employees empowered with the information they need can greatly influence the profits of a company. There are also indirect benefits incurred through happy customers.

There are plenty of companies in between, of course. Let's call them the "Bad". So, between the Good, the Bad and the Ugly, profits are certainly not shared equally. Imagine a hypothetical company in the "bad" category valued at $100m earning $5m for its shareholders, versus an otherwise identical company earning $13m for the same period. It's statistics, of course, and just as there is no such thing as a family with 2.4 kids, no two companies are identical. However, the Gallup Organization clearly shows a direct correlation between employee engagement and profitability.

You still have to close deals, win markets, develop products, and execute generally, I am often told when I bring up the topics of employee engagement and internal communications, but internal communication affects each and every one of those activities. You simply can't execute if the left hand doesn't know what the right hand is doing.

Customers always get it

The effects of poor employee communication on customer support is usually the easiest to explain, even though it might not be the most influential on profits. When customer support staff are unaware of product issues, a product might end up being returned instead of fixed with a simple over-the-phone remedy. Or reaching out to customers before they themselves discover a problem already known to the vendor can instill a sense of trust in customers that can't happen if the customer support is left in the dark. Billions of dollars are invested in customer support efficiency systems every year and yet, companies the world over neglect to connect their product groups with their service groups.

For me, the most interesting part of company operation is how it connects to its customers. Mae West gave this piece of advice to any woman who wanted to marry a divorced man: first go have lunch with his ex wife. Similarly, if you want to find out what's in store for you when dealing with a company, go talk to their customers. They know everything you need to know about what to expect.

Do you want your front line employees to be truly engaged? Give them the information they need. You can do that with an internal communications solution, and it's a great place to begin because customers are where all the energy in your company comes from, and from there, it will drive the hunger for connectedness to every corner of your company.

See more at: http://about.pdpsolutions.com/blog/employee-engagement-the-good-the-bad-and-the-ugly.shtml

26

Employee Engagement and its Link to Double-Digit Growth

Even a few percentage points difference in annual growth can decide who the leader is in your space.

FIRST PUBLISHED OCT 14, 2013

It's certainly no harm to provide to your employees a place of work that is exciting, engaging and that lifts everyone's spirits every day, but for-profit companies are not meant to be pleasure cruises. Neither do they exist simply to make life better for employees. The truth is, it's very much in the profit interests of a corporation to have engaged employees.

Consider the findings in this comparison report on single-digit growth companies (SDG for short) and double-digit growth (DDG) companies by Hewitt Associates in 2004. It shows a marked correlation between higher earnings and higher levels of employee engagement. In a nutshell, the more your employees are engaged, the more profitable your company is.

Even a few percentage points, when compounded over time, can have a profound effect on the long term growth of a company.

You might say, is it really worth the effort? What's the difference between 9% growth and 12% growth? A manager could be forgiven for believing it's hardly worth it, to make an effort to raise the numbers up a few meager points. After all, if the company is profitable, why rock the boat! Well, there are two answers to the question, each of which spells out just how big a difference it makes.

A company, by its nature, ties up an amount of capital in the hopes of increasing the value of that capital. And that process takes time. Even a modest company life of ten years would grow from $1m to $2.36m approximately, with an annual growth rate of 9%. Increasing growth from 9% to 12% would raise that ten-year value to $3.1m. That's 210% growth instead of 136% growth over the ten year period, a fifty percent improvement over the 136%, approximately. Clearly, and extra 3% makes a huge difference over a longer period of time.

Increased profits — all else being equal — increase your chances of survival generally. Success in business is a question of both increasing wealth and increasing the chances that the business will survive to increase its wealth. Even if the company did not spend a dime of the extra earnings, the extra cash in reserves may allow it to withstand other challenges later on.

That simple what-if scenario — supported by the most modest claims in reports on the connection between employee engagement and productivity — shows overwhelmingly that employee engagement is a vital ingredient in profitability.

When it's raining money, as it felt like it was doing during boom times, perhaps it matters less, because scrambling for the next bit of business may have given you a better return on effort than focusing on employee engagement. In such good times, employees too had choices, and there was less pressure on everyone to deliver, you could say. Today, however, companies and consumers are a lot more careful about how they spend money.

In the consumer world, the average family now deals with money management more like the generation who lived through the Great Depression did.

Companies, too, are in a more competitive world; not just because of the fallout from the Great Recession of 2008/2009, but technology advances keep shifting the ground underneath everyone.

Succeeding a little less often

One of my favorite lessons of anthropology is how the seemingly robust and hitherto successful Neanderthals died out. They disappeared simply because they succeeded a little less often than our direct ancestors did. For more on that subject, consider reading my older blog posting here on that subject.

Even taking a modest improvement of 12% over 9% annual growth, it's clear that employee engagement is a must have. Imagine what would happen if you doubled your growth percentage! Doubling annual growth — from, for example, 8% to 16% — is a more typical result of implementing an effective internal communications solution. In fact, we keep seeing it happen in companies that commit to internal communication.

If you give us thirty minutes of your time, we can show you why and how an internal communications solution can be so effective. Call us for a demo today! You won't be disappointed.

See more at: http://about.pdpsolutions.com/blog/employee-engagement-and-its-link-to-double-digit-g.shtml

27

Competitiveness: Why Internal Communication is the Best Way to Compete in Your Market

The glue that holds a team together is internal communication.

FIRST PUBLISHED OCT 12, 2013

After I cut the ribbon on my first startup company in 1994, I think I must have permanently injured my neck from all the looking over my shoulder I did. There were NDAs (Non-Disclosure Agreements, to protect one's intellectual property), competitive analyses to perform, and competitors to be watched closely. A "healthy dose of paranoia", I was told, was needed to stay ahead of the competition. It seemed wise, at the time, to watch the competition like a hawk. If we blinked, they might come and get us during the night.

Over the following decades, I learned that my focus was back to front. The real enemy was, in fact, within the walls of my own company. The real enemy was myself.

Only with tiny groups is teamwork less essential. Full sized teams require excellent internal communication, or the game is lost.

Any solid company leadership team will tell you, copying one's competitors' products is a risky approach. Without a comprehensive understanding of why a company offers what it does, a copying company risks getting the product or service mix terribly wrong. Killer products are born from a deep and thorough understanding of what's happening in the customer's world, not the competitors' worlds. You have to understand the fundamental problem you want to solve for the customer, and you may not even solve it the way the customer asks you to solve it. Well, that's all within the realm of product development, which we will tackle on another day, but for today, I want to talk about how to deal with the competition while staying within the walls of one's own company.

Getting your team in ship shape

Whether you're a World Cup Soccer fan or a supporter of the Indiana Redskins, you know the value of teamwork. Without it, the game falls apart and the other side wins. Getting the team to operate cohesively — via their internal communication — is the single most effective way of dealing with the competition.

When each of my sons advanced from three-a-side junior soccer on a small pitch to eleven-a-side soccer on a full sized pitch, I was amazed at how internal communication became important so suddenly. On the small pitch, any one star player could dribble the ball from one end of the pitch to the opposing goal single-handed. So a single "star player" on many an occasion won the game for their tiny team while their fellow players picked daisies or played a minor role on the pitch. On the full sized pitch, however, no one player — or even three such star players — could win the game. They simply had to cooperate intensely with almost all members of their team. Any one player would quickly exhaust themselves trying to win the game by doing it all themselves. Instead, they had to pass, pass, pass. Even a mediocre set of individual players could become a strong team if they mastered passing alone.

The transition from simple game to complex game necessitated delegation, sharing, enabling and many other elements of teamwork. The glue that holds all this together is internal communication.

In the transition from three-a-side soccer on a small pitch to eleven-a-side soccer on a full sized pitch, the team's reliance on individuals to secure victory was mitigated. The "risk" was now divided across many individuals; it was no longer all in the hands of one player. Actually, the risk of individual error being the cause of failure was all but eliminated. The redundancy of having multiple, interconnected team players reduced the risk of failure and increased the chances of success at every stage.

It was only as an adult that I learned this true value of a well-connected team. In fact, it's not a real team if the members are not connected together and are not communicating well. So the internal communication, in a way, defines their "team-ness".

It's the same in today's manufacturing company. It's all but impossible to compete in your marketplace without mastering the skill of passing: passing information between your team members. To facilitate that, companies use an Internal Communications solution. It's the irresistible force that even star players can't compete with.

See more at: http://about.pdpsolutions.com/blog/competitiveness-why-internal-communication-is-the-.shtml

Engaged Employees Have a Far Higher Retention Rate Than Disengaged Employees
Forcing employees to wear bowling shirts might be cruel, but they will love you for it.

FIRST PUBLISHED OCT 13, 2013

66% of highly engaged employees reported that they had no plans to leave their company, while only 3% of them were actively looking, compared to 12% and 31%, respectively, for disengaged employees. (Source: Towers Perrin 2004 European Talent Survey: Reconnecting with Employees: Attracting, Retaining, and Engaging, Towers Perrin).

You can read the full report by following the link, above, but for anyone making a living in this area, there aren't any surprises in it. It simply provides a lot of the scientific research behind what we all know to be true: Engaged employees stay longer, and are far more productive than disengaged employees.

Moral-building corporate events can be cheesy indeed, but they are popular with Human Resource departments because they are effective.

The Human Resource manager's dream

Imagine you are responsible for the Human Resources department in your company. Every time someone leaves to join a different company, you likely have another slot to fill. Maybe two. Advertising, candidate selection, interviewing, selection and negotiation begins all over again. And assuming a good hire is found and comes on board — an activity we all know can go horribly wrong — the long road of assimilation begins before reaching the point where they can become a fully functional, productive employee. As head of HR, therefore, you know the value of keeping good employees on board for longer. It makes your life much easier, and it's very good for the company.

You may have experienced the famous "morale-building corporate event". Your employer takes everyone bowling, or to an open-air BBQ, or a picnic perhaps. I've been to morale-building corporate events that would make a plane-spotting nerd cringe. Corny as many of them are, they are popular because they are effective. Usually managed by the Human Resources department, they can break down some of the barriers to communication between employees, and forge bonds in a way no other activity can. Fighting shoulder-to-shoulder in a paint-ball team can sow the seeds of a lifelong friendship, or at least the beginnings of a trusting relationship, between two colleagues.

An internal communications solution provides a foundation for the cooperation between colleagues, and between the company's leadership and its front line staff. It puts some structure around the daily communication needs of individuals so that nothing gets missed. Nothing gets missed because readership is measured and management knows therefore that messages are getting through.

In the end, it amounts to one thing: Engaged Employees stay longer. Often much longer. That reduces Human Resource costs, increases productivity and product quality, and makes life better for everyone. That is, if you don't count having to wear one of those horrible bowling shirts once a year.

See more at: http://about.pdpsolutions.com/blog/engaged-employees-have-a-far-higher-retention-rate.shtml

29

The Importance of Internal Communication to Every Business

What's the first step to more satisfied customers? It's getting your internal communications into ship shape. Here's how.

FIRST PUBLISHED AUG 1, 2013

I remember watching the movie Jerry McGuire. One line that stood out for me was the you complete me speech by the eponymous role played by Tom Cruise. He was talking to his then girlfriend, expressing to her that he was "incomplete until she showed up in his life".

In the real world, however, for a relationship to last, you have to show up largely complete. Ask any relationship counselor worth his or her salt. No customer, no prospect or other external force can really make up for a lack of having your own stuff sorted out before you come to the table. In fact, sometimes a customer experience can exacerbate a bad internal communication situation.

To connect with the outside world of customers, a company must first have its internal communications in ship shape.

For a company to succeed in the big bad world outside its four walls, it needs to have its internal communication in ship shape.

Internal communication is needed for the company's message to reach all of its employees, for everyone to be aware of the corporate values, its goals and what it needs from everyone on the team.

But that's not all. It's not just about broadcasting the message. A rock solid internal communication system has four moving parts.

1. Flow of information about goals, values direction, etc., from management to front line employees.
2. Mechanisms for measuring how messages are getting through.
3. Flow of ideas, feedback, market intelligence, etc., from front line employees to the management team.
4. Celebration of achievements from many-to-many points in the organization.

In your organization, how do you score on the above four points? Most companies who contact us for help are misfiring on all but one of the four, and some are missing all four. That's where we can help. Our PDP solution bridges that yawning gap between the management team and the people in your organization who make your product, and service and support your valued customers.

We all know that without customers a company is in trouble. In that sense, your customers do complete you. But when you first meet a new prospect, they'll notice quickly whether you have your internal communications in order or not. Call us today. We can make that happen.

See more at: http://about.pdpsolutions.com/blog/the-importance-of-internal-communication-to-every-.shtml

30

Internal Communications and Why the Neanderthals Disappeared

How did superior internal communication let our ancestors push the Neanderthals into extinction? Here's how they did it.

FIRST PUBLISHED AUG 2, 2013

In a dark cave in southern France, there are some of the oldest pieces of art ever discovered. The colored wall drawings are a depiction of what looks like a bison being hunted. Hundreds of thousands of years ago, our ancestors used visual materials to communicate with one another about how a hunt is executed. Art, perhaps the finest of all communications, gave homo habilis an edge over their Neanderthal rivals. The edge was just enough for habilis to eat, and for their rivals to starve to extinction.

That's the theory set forth by Jared Diamond in his book The Three Chimpanzees. The ability to transmit complex messages perfectly can still mean life or death to an organization. Clearly, a company going out of business is not on the same order as an entire humanoid species going extinct, but it's easy to see how the lack of good communication between members of a team can lead to ruin.

For all our vaunted communication skills, we humans still struggle with getting that essential internal communication right. We pay salaries, buy computers, rent factories, and pay many other bills, then we put the enterprise in peril by skimping on a minor cost. As my father often advised me with his old proverb, don't spoil the ship for a ha'porth of tar. (The metaphor says that a ship, presumably an expensive investment, should not be put at risk by saving a half penny by using less waterproofing tar.) And yet, many companies ignore this great opportunity to compete on the battlefield of business with the homo habilis edge.

At PDP we connect all the team members together. Our solution brings the company's message to everyone who needs it, and the leadership team gets marketing intelligence from the front lines.

The hunt is on. The only question remains, who is the better communicator?

See more at: http://about.pdpsolutions.com/blog/internal-communications-and-why-the-neanderthals-d.shtml

Internal Communications: Coming to a Workplace Near You

History is a record of improving communication. Here it is in the workplace.

FIRST PUBLISHED AUG 5, 2013

It's probably fair to say that, over the past few generations, marriage relationships improved as communication improved. During the Great Depression, it was all about survival, where each spouse simply got down to their side of the equation and little was said. The husband tried to be the breadwinner and the wife became a homemaker. Everyone knew what they had to do. Little was said of how a person might feel, or what they had a right to, or who wasn't getting what they deserved. Heck, they hadn't even invented deodorant.

Today, we are all encouraged to express our feelings, our needs, and also to respond to those of our respective spouses. We have New Age concepts such as "active listening" and "being in touch with our feelings" that enhance the quality of our relationships and empower us to build a better life.

Think about the changes since our grandparents' time! Resisted at first, the head-long drive for equal rights was, in the end, in men's interests, even though they didn't know it at first. Even though we still have a long way to go, improved communication is a cornerstone of a better deal for everyone.

It's the same today in the workplace. It might feel unsettling to open up the communication within an established company, to let employees really see what is going on, but in the end, it is in the interests of the company's leadership, ownership, customers and employees. We've moved into an era where to keep people in the dark is to keep them on the outside. And keeping people on the outside is likely to deprive the organization of their best work.

How is internal communication in your organization? Are you struggling to know where to start?

Most of our clients know there is an opportunity there waiting for them, but they don't know what the first step might be. That's where we have been able to help them. As partners, we know how to get you started, how to take those first steps towards improved internal communication, employee engagement and higher productivity.

See more at: http://about.pdpsolutions.com/blog/internal-communications-coming-to-a-work-place-nea.shtml

32

Internal Communication: Why Every Company Must Get it Right

How does precise communication affect the bottom line? Internal communication reduces risk of failure.

FIRST PUBLISHED AUG 3, 2013

I see it as one of my parental duties to correct my children's grammar whenever they make a mistake. My mother did it to me, and dammit Jim, I need to pass the misery on to my offspring.

All joking aside, what is the point of correcting a child's grammar? After all, doesn't "between you and I" mean the same thing as "between you and me"? Who cares if someone says "your great!" on one of your Facebook posts? (On that latter mistake, I often succumb to the temptation to reply with "my great what?", but I digress...)

Good grammar means good communication.

The point of good grammar is to minimize possible misunderstanding. That means, whatever you are trying to say is more likely to be understood the way you meant it, than it would be if you got sloppy with your grammar. It's why they bother to teach grammar in the first place.

On a grander scale, getting the company's message to front line staff is essential. Grammatical errors notwithstanding, a slight misunderstanding can have serious consequences, not to mention what happens when employees are left in the dark completely. At PDP, we understand how important it is to keep the lines of communication open between the leadership team and front line employees - those who connect with your customers, your products and your services.

Call us today. If you have thirty minutes to spare, let us show you how the PDP solution works today for our cherished clients.

See more at: http://about.pdpsolutions.com/blog/internal-communication-why-every-company-must-get-.shtml

Internal Communication: Pivotal to Turning Around a Rundown Company

What happens when a neglected company is introduced to an Internal Communications solution? They see the light.

FIRST PUBLISHED AUG 6, 2013

I was visiting relatives in the North Seattle area a few weeks ago. They had bought a small manufacturing company and were in the process of looking at ways they could re-engineer a lot of its antiquated processes. A big reason for the relatively low acquisition price was, the company did need some serious upgrading of almost everything under its roof. Still, it had a core business value hidden beneath the dozen years of neglect.

The stark contrast between any of our own PDP clients and this run-down company made me realize how powerful the core benefits of PDP's solution are, and how much we could help this fixer-upper business right away. If we do partner with them, I thought to myself, we might begin with revitalizing the communication lines — which looked to running at about 20% of optimal — between management and front line employees.

A neglected business looks to Internal Communication for recovery.

After going over the financials, my friend gave me a tour of their facility. They shared the employees' break room where they have a circle of TVs hanging above the heads of employees. It's something we see often when visiting prospective clients. The TVs displayed information on performance metrics, weather, company updates, accompanied by some elevator music. Some of the screen text was pretty small and hard to read. All of the content repeated about every twenty minutes.

They also had printouts of the same material available at several spots frequented by front line employees. Their quick-glance reports used color coding to denote performance levels. At least, I thought, they were making a serious effort to communicate. Rough as it was, management were keen on getting information into the hands of the folks who needed it.

It wasn't intended to be a prospect visit, but the new owner asked me, did I think the PDP solution could help?

Because I was talking to the new owners of the company, and not to a team that had let the company run down, it was easier to be candid about which problems the PDP solution could solve. Here's what I came up with:

PDP would strengthen and augment existing efforts with its tools and processes. In particular, moving from a static, one-way delivery to an interactive display, the user's experience would be enhanced. This would also give the new management team insights into how well messages were being understood by front line employees.

The PDP's interactive model would let the user choose what to view and move through the content at their own pace.

PDP's patented target display would be used to illustrate the company's own performance metrics, and allow those same users to drill down into the information as needed.

PDP puts at the user's fingertips, the ability to select, use their own discretion, consume the information, control the time frame and the metric, as well as many other features. It is so simple and yet so powerful.

I was totally unprepared for how the visit evolved into me giving a quick online demo of the PDP Solution! Perhaps that's the best kind, because the new business owner got it immediately. What appealed to him, a veteran of manufacturing, was how the PDP solution provides an interactive information solution to front line employees, raising the level of employee engagement. He didn't know such a system even existed. So, that's what you people at PDP do, he said.

Internal Communication = Employee Engagement = Higher Productivity

It was nice to hear from a new business owner willing to put all options on the table, and how they so quickly understood the PDP value proposition. The message: Engage employees, empower them to choose the information they need, and they will become aligned to the goals of the organization much more readily.

To Bold Moves!

See more at: http://about.pdpsolutions.com/blog/simple-yet-powerful.shtml

Internal Communications: Five Things Every SME Should Know

Small-to-medium sized companies can take easy advantage of internal communications. Here are five ways to get you started.

FIRST PUBLISHED AUG 9, 2013

I like to keep an eye on happenings in the UK relating to Internal Communications. I came across this great article on the subject and thought, these guys have experience.

You can get started today on your long term plans to improve internal communications within your organization.

To summarize, I have paraphrased and summarized here the five points they make regarding Internal Communications:

1. **It's not just for good news. Share the bads news too.**
   If it's all good news, your internal communications efforts will soon come across as a mollifying exercise to keep employees dumb and happy. Include honest updates on what is actually happening, and your good news messages will also have more potency.
2. **Align messages with their respective corporate objectives.**
   In the end, your company is there for specific reasons: To survive, prosper and grow. Ultimately, everything you do under the roof of your organization must feed into those objectives.
3. **Consider what messages your body language is**

sending alongside your spoken and written words.
4. **Be sure not to rely heavily on email.**
I remember working for a large corporation years ago. We used to call the use of email "pass the parcel". It became a way of pushing work onto other people, instead of actually sharing information and getting work done. So, I've learned to use email sparingly and use two-way communication wherever possible.
5. **Take advantage of technology solutions to support your internal communications needs.**
There are great tools on the market now to help you get the very most of internal communications, especially for connecting non-desk employees, who won't always have access to a corporate personal computer of their own. As they said in the lead-in to the X-Files TV show, the truth is out there.

See more at: http://about.pdpsolutions.com/blog/internal-communications-five-things-every-sme-shou.shtml

Getting the Message Through with Internal Communication

When Internal Communication needs a boost, a new line of communication can be the answer.

FIRST PUBLISHED AUG 10, 2013

We recently finished a smashing good video about the PDP solution. It was shot entirely on site at a client's location. All of the people in the production are actual clients of ours – not paid actors! It is so much fun to see how everyone expressed enthusiasm for improved employee communication.

One of the lines is that "PDP opened a new line of communication." On face value, that does seem lofty, but as I reflect on the statement, I know it to be entirely true.

Internal Communication isn't complete until the transmission is received and understood.

For instance, I watched an introductory video today on the online collaboration tool Microsoft SharePoint™. Not to pick on Microsoft – (as if what I say matters to them – ha) but what they are offering with their software is a way to "share comments without saying them". Users are simply writing things down and routing them using a tool. There's no new content being generated that's not already passing through the organization via another medium, such as email, word-of-mouth, or in some written form.

As I absorbed the SharePoint demonstration, it made me think again about how our own client described the PDP solution: a new line of communication.

What PDP allows a CEO to do is to open a new line of communication to deliver the company's message, its strategy, its successes, challenges, areas in need of focus, performance metrics and most importantly, its people! Every week. Every day! Every hour!

PDP also provides a way to include employees in what the company is communicating. It makes them a part of the team that identifies what the hot topics are. That is a powerful combination.

Finally, PDP's impact is quantifiable. Tracking the 'reads' — that is, how many people actually read the communication — each week gives the CEO a barometer to measure how messages are resonating or getting across, and which are being ignored. That too is powerful.

PDP does open a new line of communication. Want to learn how? Call us. To Bold Moves.

See more at: http://about.pdpsolutions.com/blog/open-a-new-line-of-communication.shtml

Excellent Internal Communication, and Other Habits You Never Want to Lose

Like the time-honored habit of using the shift key, once you experience good internal communication, it's here to stay.

FIRST PUBLISHED AUG 11, 2013

I was typing up a document for a project I am working on and I had a realization. Trivial though it may be, I never fail to hit the "shift" key in order to capitalize the first letter in a sentence. Never. This extra little typing stroke is a part of my routine even though my word processor would have done it automatically for me. This is a good habit I developed a long time ago and I guess I have deliberately not wanted to abandon the practice. Who knows why!

In a similar sense, communicating with your employees requires a level of discipline and commitment that are hard to adopt in the first place, much less sustain on a regular and frequent manner – like using the shift key at the start of all sentences. Discipline and commitment to action are aspects that are at the core of the PDP solution.

We provide tools and a process to clients that immediately — on the first day of their using PDP — injects discipline in workers' daily lives, and ensures regular and frequent information sharing, employee engagement, and measuring of results. Combined, all these factors contribute to improved organizational performance!

So in essence, once PDP is in place, you won't even think of not hitting that Shift key. It will be as automatic as ever.

Your communication will be an expected aspect of everyone's day and your employees will thank you for it!

To Bold Moves.

See more at: http://about.pdpsolutions.com/blog/internal-communication-habit.shtml

Internal Communications: "That's a Human Resources Thing, isn't it?"

Why Internal Communications is a lot more than just email and PowerPoint.

FIRST PUBLISHED AUG 12, 2013

What do these three things have in common? Marriage. Hiring. Landscaping.

Answer: Each is a beginning.

A marriage guidance counselor friend of mine said one of his most common observances among struggling couples is their lack of understanding about relationship maintenance. He said, it is as if they thought getting married was more like a "job completed" rather than the beginning of a lifelong process. Once they had walked down the aisle, they thought, they could relax, knowing "date stress" was a thing of the past.

The reality is, every relationship between humans is enhanced by clear and honest communication. And every living system requires maintenance.

You can spend a fortune on a fancy new landscaping project around your house. You can invest untold amounts on a fancy wedding, or scour the land for the best hires money can buy. But maintaining the relationships is what gives you the return for the long run.

I enjoyed this great YouTube video by ABT on Internal Communications. Or rather, on everything internal communications is not.

Internal Communications is about keeping communications going in both directions: From the management team to front line employees and from the front line staff to the management team. It's about understanding how your message is being received, and how well you are receiving messages from the front line.

It's more than just a HR thing. It's an everybody thing.

See more at: http://about.pdpsolutions.com/blog/internal-communications-thats-a-human-resources-th.shtml

Internal Communications: The Decisive Factor in Survival of the Fittest

Selfishness in an organization might reward an individual at the expense of the whole, but only when internal communication is missing.

FIRST PUBLISHED AUG 14, 2013

The phenomenon known as The Prisoner's Dilemma was framed by Merrill Flood and Melvin Dresher working at RAND in 1950. You can study the idea here, but let me jump right to its conclusion: selfishness pays. That is, everyone does better when everyone looks out for number one, according to the study.

Not so, according to recent study done by a team from Michigan State University, who identified a missing piece of the equation. In the so-called prisoner's dilemma, the parties were not allowed to communicate. Add communication to the mix, says lead author Christoph Adami of Michigan State University, and the prisoner's dilemma model falls apart. (I'm paraphrasing here for brevity).

Research has shown that the prisoner's dilemma model breaks down when you add communication to the mix.

Let's do a thought experiment on two modern, fictitious companies:

In Company A, the work culture encourages employees to think selfishly. Perhaps it is supported by adherence to rewards "by the curve". In other words, if one person gets a larger bonus, someone else in the group must get a reduced one. This, as well as other factors, maintain an every man for himself culture in Company A. Secrecy rules, and each individual sees himself as an outsider or separate from the organization.

In Company B, employees are given the tools and encouragement to share ideas and any other type of information that might help others in the organization make better decisions. In this culture, individual and group success is celebrated, and everyone is given the scoop on what's going on and how things can be improved. Employees view themselves as belonging to the bigger team and they feel like they are working for the greater good.

Supported too by this recent BBC article Selfish traits not favoured by evolution, study shows, it's clear that an organization with good internal communication has a better chance of survival. It allows individuals to improve their own chances by contributing to the success of the organization.

And let's face it. No company — let alone a species — can survive on the productivity of isolated individuals. Survival of groups has always been driven by how well its individuals share ideas. It's always been about internal communication.

See more at: http://about.pdpsolutions.com/blog/internal-communication-the-decisive-factor-in-surv.shtml

39

Employee Engagement: Why recognition is a key ingredient

Employee Engagement comes from the authentic recognition of performance. Just ask the Dolphins.

FIRST PUBLISHED AUG 15, 2013

Promise not to laugh. In high school, I was in synchronized swimming. (By the way it is a lot harder than you think! Moreover, you are holding your breath a lot, and upside down a good deal of the time). In my senior year, I was the president of the team which was named the Dolphins.

We used to perform in the school pool. You entered the pool area from the shower room and there was a stairwell of about eight steps to get to the pool deck. On the opposite side of this entryway was the bleacher section. From there, the many attendees sat to enjoy our performances.

As performers, during the shows, we would huddle out

of view on the stairs hoping to catch a glimpse of our cohorts performing ahead of us. Of greater interest was to listen to the audience. We always loved it when the crowd was engaged of course, or whenever there was a lot of applause for a particular group stunt or individual display of talent during a performance. Some crowds were generous with their applause; Some less so.

The applause, when it happened, was intoxicating. It made us girls want to perform at our very best when it came to our turn. This is a simple example of how recognition is so powerful in the workplace.

It actually takes very little to motivate people. Most people — at least, most people I've met in my life — respond well to authentic celebration of their contributions. They do, however, have to "hear the applause". Whether that is a call out in a staff meeting for a job well done, or a one-on-one chat where their good work is acknowledge verbally, recognition makes an impact and has staying power.

As a manager of people, getting and staying in the habit of employee recognition is one of the most significant employee engagement tools you have. And it's usually free! It just has to be authentic. Get in the habit today.

To Bold (swimming) Moves

See more at: http://about.pdpsolutions.com/blog/employee-engagement-recognition.shtml

40

Internal Communications Tools: The Sticky Way to Retain Your Productive Employees

The access to job-related information makes a good internal communications environment very hard to walk away from.

FIRST PUBLISHED AUG 19, 2013

Employee retention is a tough thing to predict. There are so many factors involved, it takes an expert to work out which employee might be vulnerable to being snatched by a so-called headhunter or an attractive offer down the street.

A far better way to deal with the whole employee retention issue is to put your employees on a diet. Yes, you heard it. A diet. But, I'm not talking about food here, but rather, a diet of good information. Employees who have to access to work-related information have a tougher time living without it when it's taken away.

An internal communications system is stickier than a plate of Krispy Kreme donuts. And just as hard to walk away from.

An internal communications solution provides employees with the information they need to get their job done. It makes them empowered, and this in turn translates quickly into higher levels of employee engagement. The reverse is also true. If you remove access to the information employees need to get their job done, their levels of engagement is certain to suffer. I'm not talking about the odd network outage or power failure that might deprive an employee access to their information kiosk, but rather, long term information deprivation, like they might experience if they go to work at a different employer.

Employees who have deep and broad access to information related to their work and their employer are simply more likely to stay with that employer for longer. They'll also be more productive, which I will cover again in another blog posting, but clearly, a place of work with great internal communication is stickier than a plate of Krispy Kreme donuts. And just as hard to walk away from.

See more at: http://about.pdpsolutions.com/blog/internal-communications-tools-the-sticky-way-to-re.shtml

Five Direct Benefits of Using a Modern Internal Communications Solution

Internal communication pays back in Recruitment, Employee Engagement, Customer Satisfaction, Employee Retention and Increased Productivity.

FIRST PUBLISHED AUG 20, 2013

It's easy to think the only benefit from an internal communications tool is limited to the personal level, helping people know what's going on, but there are several hard-dollar benefits that must be recognized. Let's look at what they are:

1. **Supports the recruitment process:**
   Technology is believed to have been the single biggest contributor to productivity gains since the 1980s. Likely, the trend will continue, so employees who are more adaptive to new technology are more likely to be your higher productivity employees, all

else being equal. Employment candidates who see that your organization has embraced technology are more likely to come on board, and to have drawn to your company in the first place.
2. **Raises the level of employee engagement:** An internal communication solution brings the very best out of employees because it empowers them and raises their levels of engagement at every level of their work.
3. **Increases customer satisfaction:** Much as human beings might believe they can cloak an internal malaise where they work, customers are often the first to feel the symptoms of dealing with service people working in a poor internal communications environment. Conversely, customers also get a good feeling from employees who live in a solid internal communications environment.
4. **Improves employee retention:** Empowered employees stay longer. Study after study has found that the single most effective way to keep employees on board is to empower them and get them engaged.
5. **Increases productivity:** We've all been there. We've worked in places that disempower, and places that empower. Do you remember the quality of work difference between the two?

When an employee is engaged — being a direct result of a good internal communications solution — they do better work, both in terms of quantity and quality.

See more at: http://about.pdpsolutions.com/blog/five-direct-benefits-of-using-an-modern-internal-c.shtml

42

Kiosks are Reemerging as a Cost Effective Component of the Modern Internal Communications Solution

Cost savings: A single employee information kiosk can service the two-way communication needs of hundreds of employees.

FIRST PUBLISHED AUG 22, 2013

I remember hearing my grandmother rummaging around her city council house muttering to herself about not being able to find her "wireless". She was talking about her radio, of course, and even that term is beginning to lose its traditional meaning today, because people can listen to the "radio" over their Internet connection, where radio waves might not necessarily be involved.

A single employee information kiosk can service the two-way communication between dozens, if not hundreds, of employees.

When I was a teenager, a "kiosk" was a place I could buy cigarettes while the vendor would look the other way. (Rules were a lot looser those days but let's not go down that particular rat hole today). That term — kiosk — is shifting again. Today, the term kiosk has an additional meaning, especially in the context of an internal communications solution. It now includes a vehicle for employee information distribution and collection. So, instead of giving every employee a laptop and/or a Blackberry™, a single employee information kiosk can sustain two-way communication among dozens of front line employees, their managers and their managers' managers.

Long before I ever started smoking cigarettes — as far back as the 13th century in fact — a kiosk was a kind of small, garden pavillion. It was around the time the Ottoman Empire. (Seriously. Look it up).

Now we have a new meaning for the word kiosk. Just like the term wireless, modern technology has breathed new life and meaning in the ageless physics of an old concept.

So when someone tells you they're heading to the kiosk, they are more than likely going to indulge themselves in some fresh information.

See more at: http://about.pdpsolutions.com/blog/kiosks-are-reemerging-as-a-cost-effective-componen.shtml

Internal Communications and Why Leading Companies Embrace it

Why are employees, once they've used a great internal communications system, reluctant to work without one?

FIRST PUBLISHED AUG 23, 2013

I recently handed over my ten-year-old Acura to my teenage son. In its place, I bought another used car of about the same age, to cover the few miles I drive every week. The first thing I noticed was, the replacement car did not have an outside temperature gauge, and it dawned on me just how often I had used that little information feature in the old Acura. Knowing if it was below freezing was in fact a safety feature. Even after a year-and-a-half, I still have not gotten used to not having that information available.

For over a decade of my software development career, I was focused on reporting and information systems, and for one decade in particular, I worked on the information dashboard relating to the success (or otherwise) of data backups. What I learned from that experience was, once people had access to real information related to their job, they were loathe to do without it later. The 'intelligence' of knowing what was happening in their place of work quickly became a contributor to their productivity, empowerment and perhaps even safety!

Driving a car is all about knowing stuff

Once people get used to using information to help them do their jobs, it's hard to go back to living without it.

Even driving a car to the store requires many pieces of information. A light and a buzzer warn us if we've forgotten to use our safety belt; the rear-view mirror tells us what's happening behind us. The side mirrors warn us of potential hazards to changing lanes; countless instruments tell us about our speed, engine behavior, signals, lights and — if we have a navigation system — information about our actual journey.

When we first learned to drive, it was a challenge to handle all the incoming pieces of information, but we needed all of them to drive effectively and safely. Not just lots of information, but the right information and at the right time. For example, we didn't need to know the oil pressure unless there was a problem with it.

It's the same with internal communications systems used by companies. They must deliver to the front line employee the right information at the right time.

You could say, the evolution of motoring is a story of ever-increasing availability of information. As cars became more sophisticated, information needs of drivers grew in parallel. To get the full power out of each new generation of automobile, the driver needed access to an increasing level of information. Just look at the dashboard of any powerful car. The more complex the challenge, the more information is required.

More powerful cars require more information. Compare the dashboard of the Aston Martin DB5 with that of the similar-era Austin Mini.

Business today has at its disposal a vast array of productivity tools that have enhanced our ability to compete. In fact, it is the single biggest factor in the decades-long increase in productivity of the American worker. We make more reliable products, more efficiently, quicker and in greater numbers than ever before. Companies have no choice but to embrace each wave of technology as it comes to their industry and market, but in addition, the need for employees to get access to information has grown alongside it. Employees who are given the information they need to do their work are simply more productive. When they know why they do what they do, for example, their quality of focus shows up in product and service quality.

I must go now to check on my son. The tracker I put in his car tells me he's going to be late home. That's just the kind of information I need in my job as a parent.

See more at: http://about.pdpsolutions.com/blog/internal-communications-and-insatiable-appetite-fo.shtml

44

People over Processes: How Internal Communications Makes an Organization More Productive

There is a revolution at hand. Those companies that embrace the New Age of Internal Communication will be the winners.

FIRST PUBLISHED AUG 24, 2013

Just came across an article about employee loyalty that ought to make executives stop and think about their style. Not their clothing style, but rather their management style.

The next generation of successful companies will be driven by the "people" side.

Employee Appreciation builds Strong Employee Relationships through Internal Communication. That equates to Higher Productivity.

The author declares that an evolution is underway – and I couldn't agree more – driven by a growing awareness that appreciation between employees builds strong relationships, which in turn equates to greater productivity in the workplace. Clearly, this is of huge benefit to the business, and here at PDP, we call the process "building community."

The organization that was highlighted in the piece was none other than the Green Bay Packers, an NFL (National Football League) team. The writer remarked on a missing element from an otherwise pretty darn good football team*. That missing element was a sense of camaraderie among the players.

Some of the excerpts from this story make a simple argument for how manager needs to think and act in order to propel their companies to excellence:

Employees are expected to be good project managers, great salespeople and effective technicians. Leaders are expected to be strategic thinkers, business planning experts and strong negotiators. Like football, the emphasis is on functional competencies.

There is more emphasis on the people side of business with an increased appreciation for developing emotionally intelligent leaders, a workplace that supports effective teamwork and an environment that motivates employees to perform at their highest level.

Without diluting the importance of traditional business acumen, most leaders are aware that increasing their self-awareness and their awareness of how they interact with others will have a significant impact on the success of the business.

There is plenty of research cited to back up these positions so it is worth reading the whole article to gain a better understanding. The long and the short of it is this, the People side of business is gaining prominence, understanding, and importance. If you are not there yet, get there quickly.

*You have no idea how hard it is for me to say this – you know, being from Minnesota and all.

To Bold Moves.

See more at: http://about.pdpsolutions.com/blog/people-over-processes.shtml

45

Without a Foundation of Internal Communications, Human Resources Becomes Whack-a-Mole

An internal communications solution, like oil changes and aircraft maintenance, can mean life or death for the organization.

FIRST PUBLISHED AUG 25, 2013

What have these four items got in common? Antibiotics. A fire extinguisher. A needle-and-thread. A Pink Slip.

They are all used for damage control of one type or another. In contrast to preventative actions, damage control is always about stemming loss after it has taken root.

Whether you are talking about personal health, aircraft maintenance or factory floor machinery, preventative maintenance is always the most cost effective way to stay alive, healthy and remain competitive.

Damage Control, coming to a bookshelf near you

I was given a list of books for suggested reading this morning via email. At first glance, the titles all made sense, since I do live in a world of organizational communications. Digging a bit deeper, though, I realized the book titles reflected damage control more than preventative or constructive maintenance. Take a look at the first seven titles:

- Dealing with Problem Employees, 6th Edition
- The Truth About Lies in the Workplace
- Make Difficult People Disappear

- Perfect Phrases for Dealing with Difficult People
- A Survival Guide to Managing Employees from Hell
- Tame Your Terrible Office Tyrant
- How to Deal with Annoying People

My first reaction was to feel sorry for Human Resources managers, and for other executives, who spend their working day in this world of something between triage and Whack-a-Mole.

Still, I am not surprised by the booklist because I have been witness to difficult fellow employees and direct reports aplenty in past lives. As an internal communications enthusiast, though, this accentuates how hard it is to communicate effectively in an environment where there are likely some sour folks. They do not care what you say. The big question is, though, how do things get so bad in the first place?

The answer is in how long we wait before we address an issue. Do we wait until the hotel kitchen is in flames and reach for a fire extinguisher, or do we begin with fire safety training for all staff long before it happens? Do we change the oil in our car's engine every five thousand miles, or do we wait until it seizes up on the freeway?

Do we wait for employee problems to punch us in the face, or can we do something constructive in advance?

There's no doubt, when a big problem blows up, you have to deal with it. Even with excellent fire safety training, you still want an effective fire extinguisher close by, but studies show that constructive and preventative maintenance reduce costs at every level, and significantly improve productivity.

That's why today, in an ever-increasingly complex work

environment, internal communications solutions are giving employees the information they need to do their job more effectively. As well as reducing many types of risk (e.g. an employee departing because of disengagement), internal communications solutions increase productivity. Instead of burning energy playing Whack-a-Mole, informed employees are more productive, they stay with the company longer, and they provide better service to your customers. What's not to like about that!

How about your organization? Is that a hammer lying on your desk, or are you ready to bring the good word to your front line staff today?

See more at: http://about.pdpsolutions.com/blog/without-a-foundation-of-internal-communications-hu.shtml

Internal Communications Solutions: Did Someone call it Social Media?

Savvy businesses are quietly harvesting the power and productivity of specialized Internal Communications solutions.

FIRST PUBLISHED AUG 27, 2013

Some time ago, I said to my son — not without a tinge of sarcasm — "there's more to life than the Internet, you know. You should go outside and check out the real world." His reply to me was "can you send me a link to that?"

We discussed it further. He told me about how much he depends on information from the Web for school, and for connecting with his friends without having to travel across town to get the answer. The word friends he told me, has a broader meaning than what it meant to his father's old geyser generation. More than owning a motor car or growing a set of Elvis-like sideburns, being Internet-savvy is a matter of survival for the modern teenager. In particular, exchanging information with fellow students is critical to his grades, he told me.

Ask any teenager. How much harder would it be to get school work done without any access to the Internet?

How did we ever survive, as teenagers, without that level of digital connectivity? The truth is, we did survive. We survived perfectly well without the Internet because none of our peers had access to the Internet either, so its existence was never the cause of anyone getting left behind. Today, however, I pity the poor child who has no 'net access. Everything they do — especially when it comes to information sharing for school work — would take the netless student longer, or would not happen at all.

True, Social Media can become an obsession. Just like sugar, chocolate, jogging, television, shopping and vitamin supplements, Social Media can get out of control in a person's life. But with just the right amounts, such things can be life enhancing.

A new force is quietly creeping up on the sleeping

In modern businesses today, an equivalent "force" to Social Media is being used behind the scenes. Employees have access to a new tool set that helps them get their job done, enjoy their work more, get the information they need, become more engaged and as a consequence of all of that, to become more productive. It's called an Internal Communications solution.

When the first Social Media communities emerged

(MySpace, Friendster, etc.), some companies out there actually tried to use them for their respective businesses. Business owners' instincts — that there might be some hidden value to be tapped — were right, but one-size-fits-all Social Media platforms quickly grow out of control as employees drown in information they don't need, and run out of what they do need.

Business-focused internal communications solutions give front line employees the information they need to get their work done. The 'category' came of age around 2010, and now, companies that don't take advantage of them risk being that unfortunate kid at school whose parents told him "this Internet thing is a fad."

See more at: http://about.pdpsolutions.com/blog/internal-communications-solutions-ive-heard-it-cal.shtml

How Internal Communications is the Gift that Keeps on Giving

Employee recognition through Internal Communication increases productivity further.

FIRST PUBLISHED AUG 28, 2013

People naturally want to be productive. They want the opportunity to excel, and because we are human, we also like a little recognition for it. It's why Paul Krugman of the New York Times still likes to put his name on each of his articles. It makes people listen to him when he's at cocktail parties. So, when our contributions go unnoticed, or are muddled up in a sea of confusion about who put the work in and made things happen, we become disengaged. After all, what does it matter if I do a mediocre job, save my energy for my own kitchen remodelling project, when no one will notice what I've actually achieved in my day job? That's what happens when internal communications in the workplace is broken.

A functioning internal communications system in the workplace provides transparency. Everyone gets the information they need to do their work, great ideas reach those who can execute them, and everyone knows when and by whom great work is done.

I remember being celebrated for a software project I turned around at a previous employer — it was Microsoft in 1992 — but I have, by the way, no memory of how much I was getting paid at the time. The encouragement spurred me to learn about how and why the project went so well, and to invest further learning into those areas. That, in turn, bore more fruit, and the cycle continued. Celebrating employees' successes gives you more of the same: more successes. And to celebrate employees' successes, you need rock solid internal communications. Internal communications is, as it were, the gift that keeps on giving.

See more at: http://about.pdpsolutions.com/blog/how-internal-communications-is-the-gift-that-keeps.shtml

48

Internal Communication in the Workplace: Will the Real Team Members Please Step Forward

Without solid internal communications, all employees look alike. With it, productive employees shine like diamonds.

FIRST PUBLISHED AUG 29, 2013

I suppose I am a cup-is-half-full sort of guy, but I have always believed that when people enjoy what they do, and get a little recognition for it, wonderful things can happen. Everyone is good at something — or perhaps several things — and it's much easier to find out what that is, than to force a person to perform well doing something they might not be cut out for. Still, the devil is in the proverbial details, and sometimes it takes a minor tweak to discover what a person's true skill is and unleash great works from within them.

No surprise: People with access to information about their job are more productive.

In today's workplace, life can get complicated. Tools and technology are advancing it seems faster than ever. As a technology worker myself, I live with this ever-changing smorgasbord of new ways to get things done, and I too struggle some days to keep up. (Just the other day, Google changed the default Google window by moving links to the top right, and pushing my 'News' link behind an icon. So again, I have to adjust my orientation. Darn!)

The huge productivity gains enjoyed by American industry since the 1980s, I have been told, are a result of advancing technology. Making that happen, though, were people who stepped up and learned how to use embryonic technologies. Some became cynical from frustration, while others seized each and every opportunity. Mostly, though, it was a question of just knowing that little piece you needed to know to take full advantage of a new technology wave. And to give each and every employee that advantage, an internal communications solution is imperative.

Make it easy for your employees to take advantage of every new development — and thereby raise productivity, by the way — by giving them an internal communications that they, too, take ownership for.

See more at: http://about.pdpsolutions.com/blog/internal-communication-in-the-workplace-will-the-r.shtml

Asabiyyah - The "glue" that is Internal Communication

Asabiyyah, or "social cohesion" is a centuries-old concept that plays out in the workplace today through internal communication.

FIRST PUBLISHED AUG 31, 2013

You can dig into its details on Wikipedia, but Asabiyyah is an ancient concept relating to social cohesion during the life of an organization. Paraphrasing, I'll just say that it's the essential ingredient of any organization — particularly those at the growth stage — if the organization wishes to live long and prosper, as Mister Spock might put it.

Asabiyyah is the social cohesion that makes an organization much stronger. It's the invisible force that gives its members that exciting energy to make all things possible.

Have you ever worked in a place where you could feel that energy? I have. Several times.

Asabiyyah is about connectedness. It's about a team of people having a common purpose, where the left hand knows what the proverbial right hand is doing, and where each member knows what their contribution is and why they are there.

The concept of Asabiyyah was "discovered" by Ibn Khaldun in the 14th century. He said the strength of Asabiyyah is most prevalent in the formative stage of any civilized organization, and fades as the organization becomes more bureaucratic in its waning years. Interpreted in a modern context, it's why — and this, to me, is the most interesting aspect of the phenomenon — big companies die, even with buckets of cash on hand and great apparent power over their domain. They're missing Asabiyyah.

If Ibn Khandun were alive today, he'd likely give a supportive nod to those organizations who embraced the true power of Asabiyyah with a modern, Internal Communications and Employee Engagement solution.

See more at: http://about.pdpsolutions.com/blog/asabiyyah---the-glue-that-is-internal-communicatio.shtml

50

Employee Communication and Industrial Secrecy

The chief ingredient of Employee Communication is the Why behind the many decisions made by the organization.

FIRST PUBLISHED SEP 7, 2013

One of my favorite topics for this blog is Industrial Secrecy. How do you know what to share with employees and what to keep hidden? It's a tough question, because information is power, and we want our employees to be empowered. Empowered = Productive. On the other hand, we'd prefer our competitors not to know how and why our best processes work, or what our cost structure looks like. And then there's the whole issue of secret formulas (think Coca Cola) and jealously guarded product designs.

When I started my very first company in 1994, I did worry that my brilliant ideas might be pilfered by the competition. As I gained experience over the next decades in making companies work, however, I realized more and more that even if someone stole an idea, the would-be thief would still be missing what I call the 'decryption key' to anything they stole. That decryption key is the Why. They wouldn't know why a product was designed a certain way. The why behind any process, product or service is the decryption key to knowing how to built it properly, how to use it, and perhaps most importantly, what to do next.

Mythology has it that the Soviets dismantled a DC-10 they captured in Kabul airport when they invaded Afghanistan in 1980. They failed to exploit anything they gleaned from taking the aircraft apart.

Any parent will tell you, a photograph of one of their kids tells someone very little about that child. Parents have an inimitable understanding of their own children. The same principle — on a different scale, and in a different realm, of course — applies to products and services.

When the Soviets invaded Afghanistan in 1980, a DC10 which was not able to take off in time was nabbed by the invading forces. The plane was taken back to the USSR, dismantled and copied. In the mistaken belief that by having a fully working unit of a modern, wide-bodied passenger jet in their hands, they could bring their own passenger jet line-up to the level the West was as the time, the Soviets created a complete flop. The plane they produced did look like a DC10, but performed so badly by every measure that's important in a passenger jet, their knock-off model was soon scrapped.

The reason that the attempt at copying the DC10 flopped is simple. The Soviet engineers — and I understand they put their best people on the job — didn't know the why behind any of the millions of engineering decisions that were made when designing the DC10 in the first place.

There are plenty of examples like the Soviet / DC10 story, including how companies try to copy Apple's iPhone, decrypt the Wehrmacht's Enigma machine in WWII, and many more.

The Why is the Decryption Key

Without knowing the why behind industrial decisions, facts don't carry the same value. In fact, they might actually be valueless or even distracting.

When employees are aware of why they do what they

do, when they understand the decision process behind why, for example, the large parts of a customer order are molded before the smaller parts, they are in a position to enhance the process and the final product at every level and at every stage. When employees know the why behind the stuff that happens at their place of work, they become more productive. Much more productive. An effective internal communications solution provides them with all the whys they will ever need to make that happen.

See more at: http://about.pdpsolutions.com/blog/employee-communication-and-industrial-secrecy.shtml

Give Your Employees Careers. Not Jobs
Upgrading an employee's job to a career begins with the employer.

FIRST PUBLISHED SEP 14, 2013

I watched a funny video of the comedian Chris Rock this morning. It was about the difference between having a career and having a job. He joked about how time drags when you have job, and how the day flies when you have a career. He also strongly suggested to those of us who do have a career, not to brag about it in front of those with a job.

It all got me thinking about how to change a job into a career. That is, if your employees feel they have a job, how can you help them make the upgrade? Before we dive into how that might be done, let's look at what a job is.

A job can be like being in a sort of prison. You don't like the work and you suffer your way through the day, and the five o'clock bell seems forever away. Every workday feels like

Monday, the workweek drags as if time stands still, and the weekend flies past like a runaway train. You use terms like "humpday" instead of Wednesday because the workweek feels like a huge mountain you have to climb over. You overspent a bit when you purchased that new car because, dammit, you needed some treat to compensate for the drudgery of the job. But now, the new car payments feel like an albatross around your neck, tying you to the job even more.

A career, on the other hand, feels a lot different. It might even involve the same actual work as the guy with the job, above, does, but with a career, you have a sense of belonging, ownership and empowerment in your everyday work. You jump out of bed in the morning, energized by the knowledge that today again you are going to make a difference. You know why the products you work on are built a certain way, and every time you achieve a positive result, it seems like management always notices and lets you know.

Can you imagine the difference in production quality between the guy with the job and the guy with the career? Which type of employees would you prefer to work with your customers, on your products, delivering services? The work itself is the same. It's all about a frame of mind, and it's not that hard to convert your employees' jobs into careers. Here's how...

Keep employees in the loop. Communicate with them regularly about why their work is important. How are the products produced by your employees used by customers? Why are they made a certain way? Explain to them why their work is important, and where it fits into the big picture of value delivered to customers.

Listen for new ideas. Front line staff, in a way, have

extraordinary power. They hear first hand from customers, work on your services and products every day, so naturally, that's where most great ideas come from. Keep a strong two-way connection to your front line staff to keep your finger on the pulse.

Celebrate every win. Every time a customer expresses satisfaction with one of your employee's work done, make some noise. Even if all you can do at the very moment is walk to the production floor and thank the employee in person. Everyone — from the CEO to the front line staff — needs to hear the good news when it happens.

If you want to upgrade an employee's job to a career, begin with the why, and celebrate every small win.

See more at: http://about.pdpsolutions.com/blog/give-your-employees-careers-not-jobs.shtml

Human Resources' Greatest Value may be in Introducing an Internal Communications Solution

Human Resources is often considered a Cost Center, but it can turn a troubled company into a profitable one.

FIRST PUBLISHED SEP 15, 2013

If you make a living working in HR (Human Resources), you're probably familiar with the feeling of never quite having enough budget to achieve what you have on your plate. The management team always wants more for less, and you're constantly trying to squeeze the last drop of value out of your fixed budget. If times are hard, a misguided management team may elect to cut the budget of the Human Resources department, precisely when the need for good HR practices are at their most critical.

The Human Resources department's central function, it is generally accepted, is to hire the best staff possible for the money available. That is changing, however. As organizations get more complicated — mostly as a result of technology — the power on any given individual grows. That power can be destructive just as easily as it can be constructive. Because of the leverage technology offers a company in this era, a disengaged employee can have a disproportionate ability to do a lot of damage. Sometimes it is accidental (remember the Exxon Valdez) and sometimes it is deliberate (remember Bradley Manning). Without getting into the politics of it all, large scale technology allows individuals to wreak havoc far beyond the usual power of a single pair of hands.

A disengaged employee may not be bent on bringing down the government. They might simply feel they do not belong to the organization they work for. Perhaps they simply don't care whether your customers are happy or not. Perhaps they never even think about the quality of their own work because management doesn't seem to care. After all, they haven't spoken to anyone on the management team since they first got hired. No one every patted them on the back for a job well done, but then, no one ever challenged them to do better, either. Why should they care, when no one else seems to care!

The truth is, you have an employee because the business needs that employee. And if something is important to you, you take care of it. Taking care of an employees means three things:

Staying in touch: Many — perhaps most — companies leave their employees in the dark. They don't share information that would help employees understand why their job is important. Start sharing today.

Listening: The best new ideas are in the hearts of engaged employees. They will share them with you if your feel they are part of your team.

Showing gratitude: It is said that gratitude is one of the most powerful forces in the universe, a point with which I agree. You don't have to shower a productive employee with hundred dollar bills to make them feel appreciated. It might be simply a case of walking to their workplace and shaking their hand while you say thanks.

Just as technology has changed the leverage every employee has over their domain, so too has technology enabled internal communications solutions to address all three linchpins of employee engagement.

But for today, think about the first free steps you can take to get your employees engaged. go to the front line and shake a few hands. I already told them to expect you.

See more at: http://about.pdpsolutions.com/blog/human-resources-greatest-value-may-be-in-introduci.shtml

Do your Employees Hate You? Internal Communications offers a Path Forward

Negative feelings from the front line are more often than not a call for gratitude.

FIRST PUBLISHED SEP 16, 2013

I can't remember where I heard it, but someone told me once, ninety percent of people leave their job because they don't like their boss. Perhaps that's how the statistics appear if you simply ask people why they left their job. It's often the final summary judgment of a job gone wrong. That's really what I want to talk about today. How does a job go wrong?

When my kids were younger, I remember the first time I heard those heart-piercing words "daddy, I hate you". It wasn't long before I got a grip of myself and replied "No, sweetie. You just hate how you feel".

Once as a manager many years ago, I had a departing employee sit in my office for forty-five minutes explaining how everyone in the company (all 75 of them) hated me. When I tell people that story, they usually ask why I didn't throw him out of my office. The truth is, I was intrigued by the man's gall, and I was curious enough to learn from the experience. In a way, the 45-minute monolog was an endorsement of the company's ability to take feedback from front line employees, but even if what he said was partially true, it was clear, we had a lot of disengaged employees on board.

Without knowing then what I know now about internal communications solutions, I at least determined to stay more in touch with individuals up and down the organization. In particular, I always looked for opportunities to applaud any individual's good work when I learned of it, because it's hard to be critical of someone who just thanked you for a job well done. I didn't know it at the time, but that single approach — showing gratitude for work well done — is perhaps the central most effective way to get employees reengaged.

These were the personal reminders I set for myself:
- Always show gratitude to employees for work well done.

- Never take anything personally.
- It can be a good sign that an employee is comfortable expressing dissatisfaction.
- Being a manager is not a popularity contest.

So when you learn that an employee "hates you", remember that they may just need to hear from you that they're doing a good job.

See more at: http://about.pdpsolutions.com/blog/do-your-employees-hate-you-internal-communications.shtml

Employee Engagement and Owning Your Culture

Owning your organization's culture means having an effective, two-way employee communication system to support it.

FIRST PUBLISHED SEP 8, 2013

Last night I watched one of my favorite movies — Castaway — one more time. It's a perennial human message about just how nigh impossible it is to flourish when a human tries to go it alone. Survive, perhaps. Flourish, no. The human condition is predisposed to working in teams, collaborating and communicating every inch of the way. We evolved over millions of years to be like that.

In western culture, the individual is often celebrated over the group. Captains of industry are individuals. It might be Bill Gates or Oprah Winfrey, but our media driven culture would have us believe that the stalwart Mister Gates did it all singlehandedly. In truth, there was and still is a huge team behind each of these individuals, and many more like them, each having untold numbers of people working together intensely to make it all happen.

What so-called captains of industry each managed to do was, create a new culture of communication, grow it and own it. They didn't wait for the culture to spontaneously come of age on its own. They breathed life into the culture exactly how they wanted it to be.

A productive working culture is one in which the leadership team takes an active and effective role. Nothing is left to chance, and when issues surface, management looks first to itself for the reasons why. Are we missing something? Does a process need to be improved? Where did we slip up? Self examination is a core characteristic of a leadership team that truly owns its culture and takes responsibility for what happens as a result of it. Owning your culture means being connected with every part of it, especially with front line employees. And that connection is made using an internal communications solution. Your front line employees receive your message loud and clear, and perhaps more importantly, you can hear directly from your front line employees. After all, that is where all the really good ideas come from.

See more at: http://about.pdpsolutions.com/blog/employee-engagement-and-owning-your-culture.shtml

The Holy Grail of Internal Communication: Knowing What to Focus on
Only effective internal communication can deliver what business leaders value most.

FIRST PUBLISHED SEP 6, 2013

I was struck by something I heard on the radio this morning. It was a quote from Bill Gates, and it was a rare, unequivocal vote of confidence for the late Steve Jobs. Paraphrased for brevity here, it went like this: "Steve Jobs' ability to focus in on a few things that count ... [is] amazing".

That's quite a ringing endorsement of his archnemesis, suggesting Mr. Gates really does value that particular skill in a business leader. And who wouldn't! Deciding what to focus on is about knowing "the difference between gold and fools' gold". It comes from training, experience, talent and knowledge. Jobs had all four qualities in spades, of course, and with it he has earned his place in history. For the rest of us, however, it would be difficult to step into Jobs' rather large boots. But then, building the next Apple is an unusually high goal to expect of anyone. You and I have more modest goals, perhaps, but still daunting in their own way. It's impossible to create talent, of course, and we can't increase our education and experience quickly. So we're left with the fourth ingredient: Information.

You've hired the best staff you can afford. They're educated and experienced, and if resumés and references are to be trusted, you have a team with great talent. The last substantial factor is information. But it's not just the information your employees have to help them be more productive. You also need information: You need new ideas, insights into gathering trouble spots, knowledge of chronic problems, and a general handle on your customers' experience of your product and services. Without that, decisions will be made in a vacuum or at least on outdated information. That's why the emerging business category of Internal Communications Solutions is becoming so important in business today. It's the one ingredient you have immediate control over, and it can have a profound impact on employee engagement and productivity.

Looking at how the return of Steve Jobs to Apple changed the course of technology history, you have to wonder how Bil Gates must have scratched his as he watched Jobs steal the limelight. Jobs was able to deliver his vision all the way to the employees who were tasked with executing it, and he was able to capture the hearts and minds of his target market so perfectly. The result: a series of blockbuster products that changed history.

Steve Jobs was clearly a genius, but his genius may lie in his dedication to gathering information from the front line and mixing it with his talent, experience and training to produce something extraordinary. If it were only his talent that mattered, Apple would only have had one employee.

You may not have the lofty aspirations of Steve Jobs, but effective internal communications may help you know what the "few things that count" — as Bill Gates put it — are. And when you discover that, you'll always deliver the right message to your employees on the front line.

See more at: http://about.pdpsolutions.com/blog/the-holy-grail-of-internal-communication-the-knowl.shtml

56

Engaged Employees Six Ways to Get Your Employees Engaged Again

Want to get your employees back on their game? Here are six ways.

FIRST PUBLISHED AUG 4, 2013

We're a long way from the Industrial Revolution. Back then, all you had to do is tell the employee what to do, then sit back and watch the factory hum. It's a little different today. Workers are more educated, more tech savvy of course, their expectations are high, and they can be super productive because of those factors and more. The challenge is now, how does an employer get access to that productivity potential? It's no longer even a question of the carrot or the proverbial stick. Today, employee engagement comes from the inside. That is, from within the employee themselves, and it's mostly in the form of creative energy. So, how does an employer — or a manager, for that matter — bring that energy to the fore?

1. **Empowerment**: Studies have found time and again that employees who feel they are involved in the decision making process stay longer, are more productive, and have a correspondingly positive effect on the people around them. Find ways to let employees make decisions about their day-to-day work.
2. **Celebration**: Acknowledgement of employee and team achievements have a positive and reinforcing effect on good performance. You don't have to break out the Champagne every Friday, but employees

need to know their good performance is recognized.
3. **Time out**: Getting the staff away from the work place and somewhere they can socialize together can help them empathize for each other and support their colleagues when on the job. I've been on bowling outings, paint-ball shoot-outs and lots of other corny venues. They all help.
4. **Forgiveness**: Not all new ideas work. In fact, the vast majority don't. But, you need a source of ideas in your business, and that source is likely going to be the employees on the front line. An employee may come up with a dozen ideas before a great one emerges, and it usually doesn't hurt to look at each along the way. Keep that idea channel wide open by forgiving those ideas that don't make it.
5. **Openness**: Employees who know what the company is planning on doing and who know what role their job plays in that big plan are more productive. Let your front line staff know what's going on, why their job is important, and what's happening next.
6. **Opportunities**: Let your employees know — and follow through on it — that employees will get the advantages of new opportunities in the organization. Consider "hiring from within" as a way to send a clear message to existing employees that there are ways to move up.

Notice that money and benefits aren't on my list? That's because money doesn't play a central role in employee engagement. You do still have to have a good compensation model, but once that is squared away, employees focus every day on the more ethereal aspects of life on the front line.

The PDP solution speaks to the foundation of employee engagement: Internal Communication. Call us today and see how we have helped our cherished clients bring the very best out of their employees.

See more at: http://about.pdpsolutions.com/blog/six-ways-to-get-your-employees-engaged-again.shtml

Employee Engagement and How to Become More Competitive
What would keep your competitors awake at night? Knowing you are doing this.

FIRST PUBLISHED AUG 7, 2013

In a former life, I was an executive of a high tech company. I was also a co-founder, a director, an officer, and a major shareholder of the same company. When it came to making big decisions, it was hard for me to sort out whose hat I should be wearing. If I made a decision that was self-serving as an employee, it might be in conflict with my duties as a shareholder or officer. If I looked after my shares, I might be shortchanging an employee. To say the least, there appeared to be a conflict whichever hat I wore. So, I came up with an acid test that worked very well. Whatever decision needed to be made, I would ask myself, which choice would keep my competitors awake at night? Inversely, what would I like to learn was going on in my competitors' hallways?

My answer is Internal Communication. I'd like to learn that my competitors were not communicating well inside their own company.

"God went down and confounded their speech ... and they stopped building the city."

Don't make me come down there

I'm not overly religious or anything, but the story of how God reportedly stopped the builders of the Tower of Babel in their tracks by shutting down their internal communication fascinates me. He didn't have to destroy their fancy engineering project. He simply had to shut down their internal communication, and the project stopped in its tracks.

The reverse is also true. Teams for which internal communication is enabled always do better. They build better products, better services, get more done in the same time, and increase productivity in every way imaginable.

See more at: http://about.pdpsolutions.com/blog/employee-engagement-and-how-to-become-more-competi.shtml

Employee Engagement: Why Alan Watts' Perspective is Right on the Money

How come engaged employees care less about money and more about the work? This is why.

FIRST PUBLISHED AUG 8, 2013

I stumbled over a video narrated by Alan Watts on doing what you love instead of doing what brings the most money. In a nutshell, it's another take on the adage that success comes from happiness, happiness does not come from success.

It reminds me of a truth I have come to discover in the

area of Internal Communications and Employee Engagement. When employees are empowered to make decisions in the place of work, when they are trusted to bring their creativity to bear on the problems and challenges they face at work every day, productivity increases. What's more, stress is reduced, employee retention improves, customers are better served and happier, and the organization does better in every way. There is simply no downside to improving internal communications.

At PDP, we've built a solution around the tenets that human beings are at their most productive when they are empowered, trusted and allowed to bring their creativity to work with them. It begins with a foundation of internal communications, and results in sustained, human-friendly, higher productivity.

Call us today for an online demo. Let us show you how we have helped our cherished clients take their productivity to the next level.

See more at: http://about.pdpsolutions.com/blog/employee-engagement-why-alan-watts-perspective-is-.shtml

Employee Information Kiosks are Here to Stay

You might not have noticed yet, but you're already using touch-sensitive employee information kiosks.

FIRST PUBLISHED AUG 16, 2013

When was the last time you took cash out of an ATM? Do you use the "reverse pinch" on your smartphone to zoom in on a photograph? Have you used an ever-more-popular product lookup screen in a department store? The list goes on. The reality is, touch-sensitive kiosk technology has become so easy to use and so reliable, it's all around us now.

The good news is, almost anyone you are likely to employ will have experience in using such devices, so when they are presented with your employee information kiosk for the first time, they will naturally know how to use it.

I was a nine year-old boy when Neil Armstrong was on the moon. It looked like I might actually get into space some time in my own lifetime. A few years earlier than the Apollo 11 mission, Captain Kirk of Star Trek fame used a flip-up communicator to get hold of Mister Spock. I didn't get into space, but the age of the flip-up phone appears to have come and gone. Science Fiction: 1, Reality: 0.

Another accurate prediction from Star Trek was the self-help, employee information kiosk. (Remember, Kirk et al were employees of the Federation). Today, such kiosks are everywhere. Did modern day product designers simply copy the apparent usage of the touch-screen equipment in science fiction, or was it simply a natural and obvious progression?

Whatever the genesis of employee information kiosks and the touch-sensitive technology they use, it looks like they will be with us for a long time.

At least, until I get into space.

See more at: http://about.pdpsolutions.com/blog/employee-information-kiosks-are-here-to-stay.shtml

60

Employee Information Kiosks: Keeping Up with the Latest in Employee Engagement

Employee engagement is also about helping employment candidates with the latest in internal communications solutions.

FIRST PUBLISHED AUG 17, 2013

I'm giving away my age here, but when I first got a job as a computer programmer in 1977, one huge attraction for me was that I would be working with new technology. Working with the latest generation of minicomputers, I felt, gave me a kind of career edge. I didn't care much about the salary (a whopping $40 a week, if I remember) but I sure did get excited about the tools I would be working with if I got the job.

In fact, the hiring manager told me later, I was the only candidate who asked to see the computers during the interview. That impressed him, and it played some part in my getting the job.

So, there are two lessons here:

Employers know that employees who are drawn to the latest technologies will have an easier time adjusting to and using them.

Employees who get to use the latest-and-greatest technologies are more motivated.

I'll talk about the first point in a future blog posting, but point number two tells us that using modern solutions to solve problems in the workplace has a positive effect on employee engagement right out of the proverbial box. In the gathering competition for the most productive employment candidates, offering them a work place that uses modern internal communications tools makes any employment position more attractive.

See more at: http://about.pdpsolutions.com/blog/employee-information-kiosks-keeping-up-with-the-la.shtml

Employee Engagement: Internal Communications Solutions are a Recruitment Tool

Offering employment candidates internal communication technology in their workplace is now considered a perk of the job.

FIRST PUBLISHED AUG 18, 2013

Employers often focus on salary as the main contributing factor to an attractive candidate taking a job offer. While it is important (an employee needs a paycheck to pay their rent), keeping the employee engaged after they start has far less to do with money than it does with the employee's day-to-day life on the job.

An employer will overpay an employee by $5,000 (per year, by the way) only to starve that employee of internal communications tools that cost a few hundred dollars per employee. The higher salary won't make up for the resulting day-to-day frustration or the resulting losses in productivity due to ill-informed employees on the job.

Motivation by cash doesn't go as far as an investment in internal communications.

Look at an investment in an internal communications solution as a recruitment and employee retention tool. On an employee-by-employee basis, the return on investment is far, far greater than handing out big salary increases. Access to information that helps a person get their job done is very hard to walk away from if ever that employee is considering moving to another company.

Make it a proverbial no-brainer, and give your employees an internal communications solution they can't walk away from. It will cost you pennies-on-the-dollar compared to showering them with cash.

See more at: http://about.pdpsolutions.com/blog/employee-engagement-internal-communications-soluti.shtml

Employee Engagement and the "Pull" Power of Employee Information Kiosks

Internal Communications solutions are powerful because they respect employees' need to manage the flow of information to them.

FIRST PUBLISHED AUG 26, 2013

If you run a business, likely by now you have heard of — indeed, you may be very familiar with — the term Inbound Marketing. Briefly, it speaks to the concept that people respond better when they control the flow of information coming to them. There are many manifestations of this in our society. Pay-per-click and on-demand media in general is eating into the markets of traditional we-tell-you-what-to-watch media viewing. And just look at how Netflix is eating into traditional TV viewership. Traditional advertising is under pressure from all sides because it is Outbound Marketing.

Have you also noticed how many fewer emails you get

these days? Ten years ago, every day I'd get a few humorous emails in my inbox from friends who had me on their joke distribution list. And they might get a few from me, too, on any given day. We all used email for the sharing of jokes. That was outbound or Interrupt-driven communication. Today, I get perhaps twenty emails a day, and only a half dozen make it into the new folder called Primary, courtesy of a new Gmail feature. All emails coming from, for example, the CEO of PDP Solutions, will always reach the Primary folder. No surprise there.

If I want to get hold of one of my teenage kids, I might be wasting my time using email, because they receive most of their communications now via other means, such as Social Media or SMS (if a would-be caller has their number). In Social Media, I am told, they have control over who gets how much of their attention, and when. And that's one reason they like to live there now.

What does all that mean? It means, we are in an era when the flow of information — because there is simply way too much of it — must also involve the receiver. In today's global culture, information receivers are far more involved in what information they receive.

That is why non-desk employees today often consider an internal communications solution a must-have when they go looking for a job. Once you've used one to get your work done, life at work is never the same again.

Internal Communications solutions give employees the ability to "pull" information as they need it. Instead of dumping a hundred emails onto their lap every day, an Internal Communications solution allows employees to play a more active role in how they receive and transmit information relevant to their work. Typically, they will interact with an employee information kiosk to gather the information as they need it. Once an employee has worked with such a solution, there's no going back. With the new level of employee empowerment, engagement and the resulting increased productivity, wild horses won't drag them away from it.

See more at: http://about.pdpsolutions.com/blog/employee-engagement-and-the-pull-power-of-employee.shtml

Internal Communication: Ask and You Shall Receive
Internal Communication empowers employees to ask for what they need to become more productive.

FIRST PUBLISHED SEP 1, 2013

In an airport departure lounge, years ago, I befriended a fellow traveller. He was a marriage guidance counsellor, it soon emerged. It was my big chance to get some free counsel, I thought, because everyone opens up before they embark upon a journey. What's the best way to keep a relationship together, I asked him. That's easy, he replied. Always tell the other person what you want.

He went into some detail — and I'll go into that in another blog — but what struck me was, how bad I was at telling people what I wanted. I grew up trained to be polite, to put everyone else's needs first. But sometimes, that can be a problem, not just for me, but for everyone concerned.

For employees doing their job every day, because of the hierarchical structure of companies, it can be difficult to voice your needs. It might simply be that you need a new version of a piece of software, or the cutting equipment on the factory floor could need replacement, but not being good at asking for what you need can get in the way of productivity, safety and employee retention, to name but a few.

An internal communications solution personalizes communication where it needs it and depersonalizes it when that is what's required. It personalizes it when it comes to showing the human side of team members by making a personnel database available for everyone to see, and it depersonalizes it by making requests for routine materials and changes simple and unobstructed.

If there is one area of internal communications that interests me the most, it is the vehicle it provides to productive employees for getting what they need. I wear my socks thread-bare before I replace them with new ones, I keep my car until it finally gives up the proverbial ghost, but I do spend money on having the best computer equipment and software I can get hold of to do my work every day. It's because I have learned from experience that the best tool set can have a profound effect on productivity. I don't have to ask my boss for it, because I am self-employed, but most employees struggle to ask for what they need to do a better job. An internal communications solution solves that problem by depersonalizing it.

See more at: http://about.pdpsolutions.com/blog/employee-engagement-theres-nothing-worse-than-an-u.shtml

64

Satisfied Employees are there to get; Engaged Employees are there to give

John F. Kennedy would be proud of this modern take on his 'think not...' speech. Engaged employees think not about what their employer ... (You get it).

FIRST PUBLISHED SEP 2, 2013

Bob Kelleher's new video on Employee Engagement caught my eye this morning. Although I'm now intimately familiar with the subject, the value of employee engagement can be hard to describe to someone not dealing with it every day.

Here are some of the positive soundbites from Kelleher's video. (By the way, you can watch the video without the sound because it is 100% visual, just with incidental music.)

- Capturing your employees' heads ... and their hearts.
- Releases 'discretionary effort', the magic dust of high performance.
- 480% more motivated to succeed.
- 250% more likely to recommend improvements.

Employee Engagement is the "above and beyond" effort they can contribute if they want to.

Along with the positive rewards of having engaged employees, its corollary is frightening. What happens when employees are disengaged? Well, the whole place may fall apart, now that you ask.

What stood out in the video was the effect of a disengaged manager. Employees reporting to a disengaged manager are four times more likely to be disengaged than an employee reporting to one that is engaged. So, as you go up an organization, engagement becomes more critical.

Over the years — forgive me if this comes across as cynical — I have noticed that employees tend to fit into one of two categories: (1) those are looking for a paycheck and (2) those who are looking to make a difference. A complete internal communications solution turns the former into the latter.

See more at: http://about.pdpsolutions.com/blog/satisfied-employees-are-there-to-get-engaged-emplo.shtml

The Relationship Between Recruiting and Employee Engagement

Obvious to some, the critical relationship between effective recruiting and employee engagement is often ignored.

FIRST PUBLISHED SEP 17, 2013

Just this morning, a client of mine told me of a manager he was acquainted with. The manager in question was asking my friend why all the people he hired were so docile and unexpressive during meetings or anywhere proactivity was needed on the job. My friend's answer was straightforward: it is because you went out of your way to hire subservient, non-confrontational types.

That's what happens when a manager doesn't have the confidence to hire the best candidates for the company's welfare. It takes time to address and correct a systemic management like that, and you can see how daunting a task it is for a CEO who has inherited such a situation. I'll talk about that challenge in a later blog post, but for now, let's move to the next critical factor in worker productivity facing the management team: Employee or Internal Communication.

Let's assume for the moment that you've done a decent job of recruiting a good team (or you inherited the team in your new position). You've been brave enough to hire people who might even be better than you are, so now you have plenty of good talent to work with. For some reason, though, many of them are disengaged, and product or service quality is suffering as a result of it. This is where the second — and equally vital — role of the Human Resources department comes in. That is, bringing out the very best of your front line staff.

It is amazing to me how much money is spent hiring and paying the very best talent available, and then that same resource is squandered from the day the candidate becomes an employee.

The equally vital factor of Internal Communication costs a tiny fraction of the recruitment and salary cost of an employee, yet so many companies waste their investment by ignoring internal communication.

Optimal hiring followed by effective internal communication gives you a connected, capable, engaged team. That, in turn, increases the chances of further excellent hiring. There may be a better way of making your business more competitive, but I can't think of it.

See more at: http://about.pdpsolutions.com/blog/the-relationship-between-recruiting-and-employee-e.shtml

66

Employee Engagement - Show me the Money

Research shows that higher levels of employee engagement translate into measurable and significant improvements in the bottom line.

FIRST PUBLISHED SEP 9, 2013

We know it's the right thing to do, to make your workplace more engaging for employees, but how does improved employee engagement translate into a better bottom line?

A short article on the subject popped up on my daily alert from PR Web this morning on the subject. Quantum Workplace did a survey on the effects of employee engagement — in companies that had and in companies that did not — and found some interesting numbers. In a word, employee engagement has a positive effect on stock price growth. It also has a negative effect on stock price growth when it is lacking.

Engaged Employees = Higher Profits

The study used a number of measures of financial success, to measure the correlation between employee engagement and the bottom line. Here are some of their conclusions:

- Organizations with more engaged employees experienced greater revenue growth.
- Organizations with opportunities for career development were more likely to see superior financial success.
- Highly engaged organizations experienced about

12% quarterly revenue growth compared to an approximately 6% drop in revenue at organizations with less engaged employees.
- The greatest effect on engagement between the two groups they measured was in the area of making employees feel valued.

You can read the entire report online, if you fill in your contact details.

Intuitively, it's easy to work out that keeping employees engaged makes sense. If nothing else, you will end up working in a nicer place every day. You might even make some new, lifelong friends as you get to discover the positive human side of the workforce in your own organization. It's encouraging to see, though, that it also makes financial sense. Still, if the money is not your direct concern, making the organization more financially successful increases the chances that it will be around for a long time. That alone has to make you feel more engaged.

See more at: http://about.pdpsolutions.com/blog/employee-engagement—show-me-the-money.shtml

Is your Employee Engagement Culture a Desert or Rainforest?

Something as simple as a regular thank you can transform your workplace culture into a positive, more productive one.

FIRST PUBLISHED SEP 10, 2013

Hey Mr. and Mrs. CEO. Does your company possess a Desert of Thank Yous or A Rainforest of Thank Yous?

A simple, weekly effort to say Thank You can transform a work culture into a productive one.

In a recent post, I talked about the philosophy of small wins, of celebrating the minute successes that we experience in our companies each day. About not waiting to celebrate only when the BIG event happens. Do you let such opportunities to say thank you slip by easily? I know it's easy to let that happen. You have to condition your mind to commit to doing it the moment the opportunity arises, or the opportunity will be lost, and so will the fleeting opportunity to engage with an employee.

I saw an innovative and simple exercise every single CEO could use to make sure this does not happen. I cannot recall where I found this tidbit, but that doesn't matter so much. Here was the simple process used by one CEO: Make a weekly recurring appointment in your calendar to go out and say thanks, checking off ten Thank Yous offered each day. In no time, you will be dancing in a rainforest of appreciation.

Gratitude is one of the most powerful forces in human civilization. Thanks and appreciation cultivate a pay-it-forward type mentality. Instead of tearing one another down at the first sign of an issue or concern, folks may very well jump on the appreciation bandwagon. Put that tickler on your calendar for next week and give it a go. At the very least, I know YOU will feel better – no matter what else comes of it.

See more at: http://about.pdpsolutions.com/blog/desert-or-rainforest.shtml

68

Employee Engagement feeds Productivity which feeds Employee Engagement

Once you have the Employee Engagement cycle working, it feeds on itself to pay you over and over.

FIRST PUBLISHED SEP 11, 2013

There's no downside to employee engagement. Well, perhaps there is some downside to that tiny minority of workers who thrive on the negative energy of dysfunctional organizations, but for the rest of us, and the organizations we work for, improved employee engagement is all good news. Once you get the Employee Engagement Cycle working, it begins to feed on itself.

When employees are engaged, they work better. I don't say work harder, but work better. It's actually easier to work when you feel engaged. It doesn't quite seem like work. It's more like a type of "play that you get paid for."

Sooner or later, in everyone's career, an employee will have the experience of being disengaged, and at other times, of being engaged. Even the most positive among us can't resist a disengaged culture forever if we by some chance landed a job in such a place. Think back, for a moment, about how it felt to show up every day when you were disengaged. The day dragged every bit as much as your feet dragged around the office or the factory floor. It's exhausting. Now, compare that to the feeling of being engaged. The day flies, you feel good about your work, and it shows in both the quality and volume of work you accomplish. You even look more attractive, and you call in sick less often. All of that translates into high productivity.

Higher productivity brings opportunities for all

As they say, a rising tide raise all boats. When an organization achieves higher productivity because of improved employee engagement, there are more opportunities as a result of the extra capital, superior product and service quality, happier customers, and lower costs. Offering bigger opportunities to employees, in turn, makes them more engaged and excited about their place of work. This further improves productivity and the cycle continues.

See more at: http://about.pdpsolutions.com/blog/employee-engagement-feeds-productivity-which-feeds.shtml

Employee Engagement - For Some, it's Still a Long Way to Go

Studies continue to show that employee engagement in the US is at alarmingly low levels, and dropping.

FIRST PUBLISHED SEP 12, 2013

My son shared this photo on his Facebook account. (100% of effort was carved up over an entire week!) At first glance, I thought it was quite humorous. Then the hidden truth began to seep in. For many people, that level of commitment is what they commit to their job every week, reflecting a deeper tragedy because of the poor employee engagement levels it represents.

Without running a bunch of numbers, that graphic pretty well sums up the sense of so many U.S. workers. By a margin of over two-to-one, there are more employees that are not engaged than are engaged. The latter group is the one that will give you a genuine 100% every day.

Knowing is one thing. What to do is another.

Some 87% of C-Suite executives are aware of how serious the issue of disengagement really is. I suspect, though, that few of that group know what to do about it.

To get your own employee engagement engine moving again, get your hands on subject matter materials and try to understand what engagement refers to and what it does not. There are interesting nuances to the term, and it is not widely understood. For instance, engagement is not the same as job satisfaction. Job satisfaction might help an employee sleep better at night, whereas employee engagement makes them jump out of bed in the morning, excited about what they plan to achieve that day.

It is worth understanding this not-so-subtle difference because it translates into potentially huge productivity improvements for your organization.

Look at your managers carefully. Make sure they understand what engagement is as well and what disengagement might be costing the business. As you hire new managers, start the employee engagement conversation as early as the first interview. You might start with the question, what have you done in previous positions to enhance employee engagement?

Think seriously about beefing up your employee communications. If there is one thing that can positively affect your environment, it is sharing information. If you can't commit yet to a significant project, consider opening up communication in smaller steps first. Consider using this list of suggested questions for employees to begin the process of discovery.

The time to take your first steps towards better employee engagement is now. The employment scene is starting to pick up energy, with staff turnover showing signs of movement. Don't be kept at the back of the pack by remaining ignorant of the impacts of employee engagement.

See more at: http://about.pdpsolutions.com/blog/employee-engagement---for-some-a-long-way-to-go.shtml

Getting the Employee Engagement Machine Moving : The First Five Steps

Changing a culture is one of the hardest things to do in an organization. The secret is to focus on one step at a time.

FIRST PUBLISHED SEP 13, 2013

If you've been handed responsibility for an organization in disarray, or if you've looked around you to discover the organization you've been leading has decayed culturally to the point where remedial action is required, you probably understand the scale of the challenge before you. That's because a culture is one of the hardest things in the world to change. Despite the challenge, there are many options available to you. And one big thing in your favor is, you're in charge. That means, you do have enough control to make the first few decisions. After that, it will get easier.

Here's my list, in sequence, of your first steps to getting your employees engaged and on the path to higher productivity:

1. **Make face-to-face contact with everyone in your organization.** If it's accepted knowledge that the culture is in trouble, talk to each person about your

new commitment to improving things for everyone, about making it a better place to work, about introducing new ways to bring employees' concerns and ideas to the people who can make changes.

This step may take a while, but it's a great investment. Shaking hands with each person in turn, introducing yourself, making a mental note of their name, and what they do every day in their job, comprises the first important step in this process.

2. **Identify likely team members of your new Employee Engagement Task Force.** They don't have to be the most agreeable of all your staff members. In fact, getting some of the more vocal or cantankerous employees on the Task Force may bring more transparency to the process. The key here is for representation from all levels of the organization with "skin in the game", as they say. (I dislike that cliché, but it's very apt here).
3. **Together, set goals.** Give members of the Task Force the time in their workweek to meet at least every other day to begin with. Decide on the goals you want to achieve. As a suggestion, start with a goal of four weeks to get a survey prepared to ask all employees what changes they would like to see most. Consider using a free service like www.surveymonkey.com to get the ball rolling. If employees don't have access to email, give them a simple sheet of paper to fill in and drop off. Keep it open-ended, constructive (e.g. Don't ask "what do you hate most about this place?" but rather "if you could make one improvement here, what would it be?") and free form so what you collect

will provide a feel for the scope of what's ahead, particularly where you see a pattern. Encourage people to focus on issues and not on individuals.

4. **Identify what preliminary tools you may be able to use to help.** At first, it might be a simple weekly one-page "What's happening at Acme Corp". Later, it might include technology that enables the process.
5. **Identify long term solutions:** This is where the use of tools and technology should be considered. Start to get familiar with what is available, with emphasis on a good match between your type of business and solution providers who already support clients like you.

That should help get the process moving. Most important of all, it must be a team effort. Simply getting a multi-level Task Force in the same room and talking with one another will yield dividends. The very fact that you're reading this short article means you're actually on your journey already.

The next step? Start with number one on my list, above.

See more at: http://about.pdpsolutions.com/blog/getting-the-employee-engagement-machine-moving-the.shtml

71

Employee Communication and Industrial Secrecy

The chief ingredient of Employee Communication is the Why behind the many decisions made by the organization.

PUBLISHED SEP 7, 2013

One of my favorite topics for this blog is Industrial Secrecy. How do you know what to share with employees and what to keep hidden? It's a tough question, because information is power, and we want our employees to be empowered. Empowered = Productive. On the other hand, we'd prefer our competitors not to know how and why our best processes work, or what our cost structure looks like. And then there's the whole issue of secret formulas (think Coca Cola) and jealously guarded product designs.

When I started my very first company in 1994, I did worry that my brilliant ideas might be pilfered by the competition. As I gained experience over the next decades in making companies work, however, I realized more and more that even if someone stole an idea, the would-be thief would still be missing what I call the 'decryption key' to anything they stole. That decryption key is the Why. They wouldn't know why a product was designed a certain way. The why behind any process, product or service is the decryption key to knowing how to built it properly, how to use it, and perhaps most importantly, what to do next.

Mythology has it that the Soviets dismantled a DC-10 they captured in Kabul airport when they invaded Afghanistan in 1980. They failed to exploit anything they gleaned from taking the aircraft apart.

Any parent will tell you, a photograph of one of their kids tells someone very little about that child. Parents have an inimitable understanding of their own children. The same principle — on a different scale, and in a different realm, of course — applies to products and services.

When the Soviets invaded Afghanistan in 1980, a DC10 which was not able to take off in time was nabbed by the invading forces. The plane was taken back to the USSR, dismantled and copied. In the mistaken belief that by having a fully working unit of a modern, wide-bodied passenger jet in their hands, they could bring their own passenger jet line-up to the level the West was as the time, the Soviets created a complete flop. The plane they produced did look like a DC10, but performed so badly by every measure that's important in a passenger jet, their knock-off model was soon scrapped.

The reason that the attempt at copying the DC10 flopped is simple. The Soviet engineers — and I understand they put their best people on the job — didn't know the why behind any of the millions of engineering decisions that were made when designing the DC10 in the first place.

There are plenty of examples like the Soviet / DC10 story, including how companies try to copy Apple's iPhone, decrypt the Wehrmacht's Enigma machine in WWII, and many more.

Without knowing the why behind industrial decisions, facts don't carry the same value. In fact, they might actually be valueless or even distracting.

When employees are aware of why they do what they do, when they understand the decision process behind why, for example, the large parts of a customer order are molded before the smaller parts, they are in a position to enhance the process and the final product at every level and at every stage. When employees know the why behind the stuff that happens at their place of work, they become more productive. Much more productive. An effective internal communications solution provides them with all the whys they will ever need to make that happen.

See more at: http://about.pdpsolutions.com/blog/employee-communication-and-industrial-secrecy.shtml

Successful Employee Engagement is made of a "Thousand Small Wins"

If the fruits of Employee Engagement are what you seek, keep a sharp eye out for the next good thing that happens.

FIRST PUBLISHED SEP 5, 2013

Any meaningful relationship, every beautiful garden, and each worthwhile life project takes time to cultivate. Just as you don't leave it to the day before your teenage child goes off to college to give them the "big talk about life", valuable relationships in the workplace are made up of countless seemingly minor events, each being paid the full attention it deserves. Together, they add up to a success story.

I was meeting yesterday with our founder/owner and once again was struck by his vision and insight into the power of communicating effectively over the years with his employees.

He noted specifically, that leaders regularly miss opportunities to leverage the "small wins", as he put it, an example of which was, "The Accounts Receivable rep who finally collected on the long overdue account. That is a small win. And yet, only a couple of people will know about it in the company, and that is a small win that should be celebrated!"

How many does your company experience in a single day? Do you have a commitment to collect, celebrate and communicate those small wins to the whole team? Do you have a communication process in place to leverage those moments – for the good of the morale and engagement of your employees? You should!

Big wins come infrequently and are usually predictable. In reality, the air is out of the proverbial tires by the time that Big Win is announced. It's usually such a big event in an organization that people have often spent all its energy by the time it comes to pass.

Small wins, on the other hand, can be more individualized, and actually more potent in certain respects. Celebrating small wins implies that the company is paying attention and values each and everyone's contributions, large and sweeping, as well as minor and important. That the details matter is as important a message to send as the event itself.

Celebration of a "Big Win" is, in a way, easy. People expect to hear a lot of noise when Phil from Inbound Sales blows past his sales quota. Certainly, Phil does. But true success for the organization is made up of many individual efforts from individuals every working day. Celebrating each Little Win makes the next one more likely. And the next one.

Keep your eye out for an opportunity to celebrate the next such "small win". It may be right in front of you.

See more at: http://about.pdpsolutions.com/blog/small-wins.shtml

73

On the Adoption and Acceptance of Touchscreen Technology
Probably 90% of people use touchscreen technology every day, mostly without knowing it.

FIRST PUBLISHED SEP 4, 2013

A recent prospect was noodling on whether their front line employees would adopt the use of the touchscreen kiosks we use in production floor areas. In the context of internal communication systems, their purpose is to put information close at hand and easy to use, as opposed to having to boot up a PC, use and keyboard and mouse to find a quick answer to a single question.

I assured the prospect that indeed employees of all ranks and ages do really like using the kiosks. Our weekly user reports show the level of reads (or the times content was accessed) using the touchscreen kiosks, so we know their adoption rate is almost immediate. In fact, without even describing how the screens are used, new users instinctively reach out to engage with the inviting new interface.

Most people use touchscreen technology every day, often without know it, but still, many folks are startled when you tell them their solution will involve the use of touchscreens. I should think we are very near to obsolescence in that line of thinking – when we will reach a time in our lives where there is nothing but touchscreen technology and everyone is more than comfortable with it.

It is like online banking. I remember the day when you would call down to the bank to make a transfer of money from savings to checking or vice versa. Now that is laughable and hard to believe we ever did it.

Not being used to touchscreen technology may soon become laughable as well. Case in point, my 1.5 year-old granddaughter will pick up my smart phone, and immediately swipe her little chubby thumb across the unlock band at the bottom and voila! She has access to all of the info on my phone. Same goes for my Kindle. She knows how to unlock that one and swipe to the Curious George videos!

Even babies these days witness their parents and other caregivers using touchscreens all the time. They are literally growing up with the technology and are more than comfortable using it. The day will come when we will not believe that people actually were averse to using these tools.

That's it for today. I have to rush away now to feed my carrier pigeons.

See more at: http://about.pdpsolutions.com/blog/on-touchscreen-technology.shtml

Internal Communication. When you are your own worst enemy

Internal Communication has been the second biggest factor in the success of startups. Second only to the quality of hiring. Here's why.

FIRST PUBLISHED SEP 3, 2013

I've spent most of my career in small companies, and most of those were startups in which I was a founder or co-founder. For the first couple, I remember having a child-like fear of competition. Secrets were to be kept, and a paranoid eye was always to be trained upon the ever-powerful competitors executing against every opportunity we exposed through carelessness or innocence. As I gained experience over the years of successes and failures, however, I learned that our true 'villain' had always between the walls of our very own company. No, I didn't discover a clandestine industrial espionage ring stealing our secrets. The villain could be seen in plain sight, simply by looking in the bathroom mirror.

I discovered that, provided the market did exist for the product or service we were offering, the path to success or failure rested entirely within the walls of the company. How did we relate to customers needs? How well did we respond to new ideas coming from our customer-facing employees? How well did we keep everyone in the loop about where the company was going? Did the right hand know what the proverbial left hand was doing?

Success is not about secrets. It's about execution on a foundation of excellent internal communications.

The only thing that was more important to internal communication was Hiring. In hindsight I noticed that every positive inflection point in the company's history coincided with the arrival of a team member. Not just any team member. What all inflection point team players had in common was this: They had each done, in a previous job, exactly what we were asking them to do in this job. That made the hiring process perhaps the Number One success factor ahead of Internal Communication, but it was because we had excellent internal communication that allowed us to work the hiring process so well.

The inverse was also true. For example, we took a very

successful salesperson and gave him the job of head of marketing. (Please don't laugh. It was a mistake, I know that now.) Marketing stopped dead in its tracks while he stumbled through the steep learning curve; we lost traction and we lost precious time. That one mistake may have lost us the game in that particular opportunity, but such is the price of experience! We made other mistakes, too, but that was one of the bigger ones.

So, you've hired a great team. They each have a proven track record behind them, and now it's a question of execution.

No sooner is each member of your dream team in the door, you begin to absorb the value of those special skills they gained through hard-earned experience. After all, the company needs to internalize that value right into its core processes and knowhow. That's where internal communication plays one of its key roles: to convert expert individual knowledge into corporate process value.

Internal Communication. Even if it is Number Two to Good Hiring, it's only because Good Hiring got there on a foundation of Internal Communication.

See more at: http://about.pdpsolutions.com/blog/internal-communication-when-you-are-your-own-worst.shtml

75

Increasing Productivity Internal Communications: Ten Free Ways to Get Started

Neglected for years? Panic not. Here are ten ways to get your Internal Communications working again.

FIRST PUBLISHED AUG 13, 2013

When someone is looking for a way to improve their internal communications, and they reach out to us, one of the first questions they ask is, how and where do I start?

So, I've come up with my favorite ten first steps. With the exception of the pizza in item 9, each is free to do, and together they will get your organization talking again, and productivity on the rise.

1. **Walk the walk**: Before you spend another moment polishing an email or scrubbing a PowerPoint presentation, stand up and walk to the people in your organization who meet with customers. If you're running a production facility, go meet the people who put the finishing touches to the products before they get shipped to customers. If you don't know them personally, introduce yourself and try to get a feel for what their day's work entails.
2. **Do some research**: If you're reading this article — you are reading this, right? — you've already taken this step. There are so many resources out there to help you decide what options might serve you best. Here is a Youtube playlist videos we produced on the subject of Internal Communications to get you started.

3. **Find out where you are**: As my father would often say to me, if you don't know where are, you're probably pointing the wrong direction. Get familiar with where you are today by taking this simple test.
4. **Make a one-year plan**: People are often afraid to make plans because they fear they will be wrong. The one thing you know about a forecast, the late Frank Gaudette (former CFO of Microsoft) would often say, is that it is wrong. But a plausible plan is a great way to measure progress.
5. **Ask for input**: As you talk face-to-face with your front line employees, ask them for their views on how internal communications could be improved.
6. **Assemble a team:** Internal Communications needs cooperation. You'll need a team of people from all levels of the organization, particularly from your front line staff.
7. **Use existing experience**: For years I've had a close friend working as HR director. Only last week I discovered she had a qualification in internal communications. Ask your staff about any previous experience or training in using internal communications tools they might have.
8. **Take an online course:** There are so many free resources out there. Start with a search of 'internal communications' on YouTube.
9. **Ask for content**: One of the most memorable experiences I ever had as an employee was an off-site session where everyone was asked to tell of a memorable work experience. Step away from the day-to-day work and ask people to open up. It might even be

over pizza and pop in the warehouse.
10. **Share ownership**: For internal communications to work in the long term, you will need buy-in from team members at each level of the organization. Loosen your grip on the reins a little and let front line staff contribute to the decision making in your new internal communications initiative.

Internal Communications is about the survival and prosperity of the organization. Start today.

See more at: http://about.pdpsolutions.com/blog/internal-communications-ten-free-ways-to-get-start.shtml

www.ingramcontent.com/pod-product-compliance
Lightning Source LLC
Chambersburg PA
CBHW051703170526
45167CB00002B/516